Praise for *Legacy Living: The Six Covenants for Personal & Professional Excellence*

"Envisioning our legacy for tomorrow can help us learn how to live today. All leaders need to demonstrate *Legacy Living* for their employees. Great coaching to help all of us focus on what really matters!"

—Marshall Goldsmith, Author of *The Leader of the Future*, a *Business Week* best-seller, World-renowned executive coach, Recognized as one of 50 great thinkers and leaders of the past 80 years

"This book is about the landscape of transformation, or as Gloria poetically frames it, 'deconstructing the armature of the heart.' The power and precision of her language and spirit give life and relevance to the book. I strongly recommend that anyone who cares about changing themselves or the world, read it."

—Peter Block, Author, *Stewardship: Choosing Service Over Self Interest* and *The Answer to How is Yes*

"Punctuated throughout with her poignant poetry, Gloria Burgess has written a beautifully elegant, yet practical book to lead you toward personal and professional excellence. She extends an invitation to explore six covenants—or promises—designed to keep you on an inspirational path to a greater vision of who you are and what you can become—all with the gentle guidance and strength of our Creator. I accept her invitation to embark on this inspirational journey and hope you will too."

—Paul J. Meyer, Founder of Success Motivation Institute, Inc. and *New York Times* best-selling author

"This inspirational book demonstrates in practical ways how to cultivate the character qualities of love, faith, trust, wisdom, vision, and integrity in order to unharness the unlimited creativity and resourcefulness found in the human spirit. Gloria Burgess provides an invaluable guidebook for any profession, age group, or individual."

—Angeles Arrien, Ph.D., Author, *The Second Half of Life* and *TheFour-Fold Way*

Also by Gloria J. Burgess

Poetry

A Yellow Wood
Journey of the Rose
The Open Door

Other Books

Living Your Creativity Every Day
Continuum: The First Songbook of Sweet Honey in the Rock
(editor)

Audio

Journey of the Rose (spoken word and original music)
Jammin'! The Soul of Leadership

Films

The Heart of Business—Across Borders Productions
Social Activism and the Arts—Public Broadcasting System

For more information on other books, visit *www.jazz-inc.com.*

Legacy Living

The Six Covenants for Personal & Professional Excellence

GLORIA J. BURGESS

For permission requests, contact the publisher at:

Executive Excellence Publishing
1366 East 1120 South
Provo, UT 84606
Phone: 1-801-375-4060
Toll Free: 1-800-304-9782
Fax: 1-801-377-5960
www.LeaderExcel.com

Gloria J. Burgess
Jazz, Inc.
E-mail: legacyliving@jazz-inc.com
Phone: 1-206-954-0732
Fax: 1-425-776-4640
www.legacy-living.com

For additional Jazz, Inc. products, please visit www.jazz-inc.com.

For Executive Excellence books, magazines and other products,
contact Executive Excellence directly. Call 1-800-304-9782,
fax 1-801-377-5960, or visit our website at www.LeaderExcel.com.

ISBN 1-930771-17-7
EAN 9781-930771-17-8

Table of Contents

In Gratitude

I thank God for ordering my steps. I'm grateful for each magnificent mountain and the terrible yet illuminating valleys along the way, and for going before me in all things.

To Ken Shelton, publisher of Executive Excellence Publishing: thank you for inviting me to send you my manuscript at a time when I'd become discouraged about finding the right publisher. To other members of the Executive Excellence Publishing team, especially to Brian Smith and Benjamin Devey: thank you for your patient, insightful support in bringing this book to life.

With deep gratitude to my African, Cherokee, Choctaw, and Scotch-Irish ancestors: you are my cloud of witnesses and wisdom council. Thank you for passing on your legacies of gratitude, service, unshakable faith, vision, courage, compassion, forgiveness, strength, hope, perseverance, triumph, passion, and joy.

With deep appreciation and gratitude to the many allies who have supported, encouraged, and enlightened me on my journey of shaping this book. I thank my faithful clients and superb students who road-tested the book through edifying conversations and workshops. I deeply appreciate your spiritual, emotional, intellectual, and creative support. Thank you: Ellen Antonelli, Carrie Applegate, Lynn Biggs, Sharon Bouscher, Julie Brockmeyer, Judith Chandler, Rebecca Crichton, Joan Dever, Kate Elliott, Nikky Finney, Lois Greenberg, Jonathan Hardy, Cheryl Hawley, Rita Howard, Sally Johnson, Erwin Karl, Margy Kotick, Dan Leahy, Ruth Massinga, Vera McEwen, John Oleson, Deb Partington, Tracy

Patterson, Constance Rice, Jane Sallis, Eva Sher, Anne Smith, Anne Stadler, Dona Taylor, Kate Thompson, Ione Turner, Evelyn Wemhoff, Donald Williamson, and Betsy Wilson.

Bronwyn and Rikki Cooke, thank you for creating the Hui Ho'olana Retreat Center, an extraordinary haven on the Island of Molokai. In the glorious, nourishing embrace of the Pacific Ocean and gracious staff at the Hui, I wrote an early draft of this book.

Special thanks to Diana Lilla, Geoff Bellman, Jeevan Sivasubramaniam, and Cyndi Crother, who believed in my book at critical stages of its development.

To Toi Derricotte and Cornelius Eady, co-founders of Cave Canem: thank you for your amazing vision and courageous commitment to providing an uncommon and necessary sanctuary for poets and writers of the African Diaspora. Each healing begets fierce, delectable warrior flowers.

Thank you David Whyte, Naomi Shihab Nye, and Kwame Dawes—kindred spirits and pioneering poets: your poetic sensibility and provocative insights continue to transform our corporate, civic, health care, and educational institutions, making these institutions habitable and more hospitable to matters of the heart.

Thank you to my family for teaching me how to be an honorable daughter, sister, mother, and friend.

To my mother, Mildred: thank you for your legacy of unflagging faith in God and in me, and for your common sense and wisdom. To my father, Earnest: thank you for your legacy of encouraging me to be true to myself and to take up my ministry, even before I knew that one could minister without a pulpit. To Annie, Deborah, Doris, and Vera—my sisters, you are astonishing allies, with stalwart souls and mighty arms of love.

To my daughter, Quinn: thank you for your abiding love, humor, and generous, effervescent spirit.

To my husband, John: thank you for your steadfast love and servant heart. I'm humbled and blessed by your many editorial and clerical gifts, especially your patience in deciphering my many handwritten drafts. I'm deeply grateful for your companionship as we continue to learn together about legacy living.

Thank you readers. As part of my legacy, I offer this book to you—for caring enough about yourself and others to transform yourself and transform our world.

Dedication

I dedicate this book to my father and mother whose legacies continue to unfold and shape my life. I also dedicate it to my husband and daughter, John and Quinn, whose servant hearts are the very embodiment of legacy living.

Prelude

Your purpose is most profoundly expressed not by what you do but by who you are and the legacy you leave behind. The question is—*how will I live my life so that I leave a worthy inheritance?* Not of money, but an inheritance that money can't buy—a legacy of the heart.

Consciously or not, each of us leaves a legacy, a trace, of our life here on earth. The goal of life and this book are the same—to be conscious of what we're creating and of what we'll leave behind as we fulfill our potential as creative beings.

The premise of *Legacy Living* is *creative equanimity*. Simply put, we're all creative. There are over six billion people on the planet, and each one of us is a unique, creative force. Being creative is our birthright. It is who and how God intended us to be.

What we do with our birthright is a matter of choice. Whether we become painters or plumbers, actors or attorneys, teachers or technicians, singers or scientists, we are called to ignite our creativity to shape the kind of world we want to live in and to leave as a shining legacy for our children and our children's children.

Once ignited, how do we sustain our creative fire? One way is to align our values and voice. When we bring our authentic voices forward, we bring forth our signature presence—our special skills, talents, and abilities that exist nowhere else on the planet. Today more than ever, each of us has a responsibility to live with authenticity, to align our values and voices, in our relationships, in our workplaces, and in our communities.

As stewards of the future, the central questions we must answer are:

1. Who am I—*really*?

2. What do I want to create and for whom?

3. How will I use my voice, my signature presence, with purpose and passion to transform myself and others?

To respond fully to these questions, this book offers practical wisdom based on six principles. I call these principles "covenants," or promises, which are at the heart of living a creative, authentic life. Like the air that sustains us, the covenants are necessary agreements, promises we make with ourselves on behalf of ourselves and others. As timeless as they are universal, the covenants inspire our devotion to a life that puts service to others above self-interest. They keep us on a path where we fall joyously in love with the future over and over again. The six covenants are: *legacy, gratitude, faith, love, vision,* and *integrity.*

Crossing

For the thousands of innocents who perished on September 11, 2001 by fire, ash, jumping, and falling at the World Trade Center, the Pentagon, and on that lonely field near Pittsburgh, Pennsylvania, and for the tens of millions around the world whose lives were forever transformed by that fire and countless others.

we stand on the bridge staring down
our resistance stunned into silence

look into the moon bright water at the face
that passes for what we used to call life

how to put a toe in test the shallows
lower the heel then the place where an arch might be

how to wrap all your belongings
pride jealousy prejudice fear even the silence

how to wrap them into netting
drop them let them sink granite like

through blue black current
diminish the strain on heart and hand

from the dark a voice cries out
calls you to lift your face to the wind

follow the cry your only light
press worried fingers into pocket linings deep fleecy warm

throw away your amulet of worn gray stones
fill your lungs with earth's new music

make way for the only thing that pulls you
as compost heaps steam promises of new life

and the only price for salvation is deconstructing the armature
of the heart making the great crossing then waiting
waiting
waiting

– Gloria Burgess

*If you do not come to know the deeper
mythic resonances that make up your
life, they will simply rise up and take you
over...the myth will live you.*

– Joseph Campbell

First Steps on the Inspirational Path

Life's journey is all about discovering (or for some of us recovering) our authentic voice. Once we find it, our responsibility is to bring our authentic voices forward. When we do so, we bring forth our signature presence—our special skills, talents, and abilities that exist nowhere else on the planet. To echo Archbishop Desmond Tutu's words, "God is waiting on us. He needs our help." God is waiting on us to bring forth our signature presence in our families, communities, workplaces, and spiritual sanctuaries.

Our journey on the inspirational path invites us to excavate and unearth our true voice. Our goal is to deepen our understanding of ourselves and use our signature presence to share joy, magic, and beauty.

Now more than ever the world needs your signature presence. The world needs your light, the magnificence of who you are. Each of us has a responsibility to use our presence, to claim our brilliance, to share our radiance with the world.

The journey begins differently for each of us. Some of us know early on what we are called to do. We know how we are called to use our creativity. If we are alert, we heed the call. If we are not alert, we are called not once, not twice, but many times before we finally respond.

Whether it is out of our own courage or sheer necessity, our journey begins when we take the first steps, however tentative or bold, that will lead us into the depths of who we really are. Expressed in the words of that old spiritual *Wade in the Water*, the journey calls us to be attentive and open to change.

> *Wade in the water.*
> *Wade in the water, children.*
> *Wade in the water.*
> *God's gonna trouble the water.*

The call to "wade in the water" is a seductive invitation and is not to be taken lightly. It is a call of the highest order. We are called to immerse ourselves—metaphorically and spiritually—in the currents of self-discovery. We are called to a rite of passage that signifies transformation.

"God's gonna trouble the water" is code language for *your life is about to be deeply changed.* Why? Because these are not ordinary waters. They are spiritual waters, and when we enter them, we say *yes* to the swirling currents of discovery. We say *yes* to the ebb and flow of faith and doubt. We say *yes* to the necessary descent into the murkiness and majesty of our own mystery. And we say *yes* to the inevitable ascent.

When we enter the spiritual waters, we enter as "children"—innocent, naive, and open. When we emerge from the waters, we are forever changed. By saying *yes* to "God's troubling," we emerge with heightened self awareness, deeper knowledge, and greater compassion, wisdom, and generosity for ourselves and for others.

When we respond to the call, we join a procession of elders and contemporaries who have waded ankle, waist, or chin deep in these same baptismal waters. We join a gathering of the changed, a gathering of those who have embodied and become the change they want to see. We join a congregation of stewards whose charge is to leave a shining legacy for future generations.

No matter how your journey on the inspirational path begins, you will encounter self-doubt and feelings of insufficiency. Feelings of self-doubt and insufficiency are a normal part of the creative process. It is a normal part of discovering and aligning your voice and values. It is a normal part of bringing forth your signature presence.

The challenge is to acknowledge the feelings of doubt and insufficiency and deal with them. Unattended, these feelings will douse your creative fire, sap your stamina, and erode your confidence. Unattended for long periods of time, you may come to believe that you are a misfit. Even worse, you might believe that you are not at all creative or unique. This is the biggest lie of all. Do not believe it. You are born to be creative. It is your birthright. In fact, if you were to deny your creativity, you would surely die. For the source of your creativity is borne of the very air you breathe, which springs from the breath of God.

Our creativity is our gift from God. Our use of it is our gift to God.

– Julia Cameron

Legacy living demands that you forget whatever lies you have been told about your creative self. At its deepest level, legacy living means listening and responding to your innermost longing. Because most of us live lives fraught with distraction and competing priorities, legacy living requires nurturing and support *every day*, the kind of nurturing that can come only from you.

Legacy living means making a commitment to yourself. That commitment means saying *yes* to what truly matters, to bringing forth your signature presence. When you say *yes*, you make a promise to yourself, the world around you, and to God.

This kind of promise is a covenant, a promise that you commit to act on. You must take action not once, but moment by moment, day by day—every single day each day for the rest of your life.

———◇———

I wrote this book to:

• Honor legacy living as a sacred commitment, a covenant that you make with yourself and to future generations.

• Offer hope and inspiration to you wherever you are on your inspirational path. It helps to know you are not alone. It helps to know that others struggle with the same issues as you, and that you can triumph just as others have triumphed.

• Offer the six covenants to nurture and support you, as they have nurtured and sustained me on my inspirational path.

• Encourage you to align your values and voice, as well as to broaden and deepen your creativity.

• Enhance what we know about creativity and its value in our lives.

• Join you in being more conscious of the creative process and its possibilities. For when we live each moment with creative awareness and intention, we participate in creating a positive legacy for future generations.

When we cultivate our awareness and intention, we begin to see with our eyes and our hearts. When we see in this way, we instinctively acknowledge our kinship with and caring for others. We also acknowledge the depths of our own creativity, the magnitude of our inheritance. As scholar Joseph Campbell

When it's over,
I want to say:
all my life

I was a bride
married to
amazement.

I was the bridegroom,
taking the world
into my arms.

– Mary Oliver

reminds us, the price of this inheritance is that "we must be willing to give up the life we've planned, so as to have the life that is waiting for us."

We wade through the currents of change to embrace the life that is waiting for us—our glorious creativity and the inherent power and authenticity of our own true voice. When lived with awareness and intention, with creative acumen, we can be confident that our singular and precious life, our signature presence, will be a felt presence in all the earth. And at the end of life, we ought to be able to say we lived in service to God, in service to our creativity, and in service to future generations. We ought to be able to say I lived my life fueled by the power of legacy, with the intention of transforming myself and the world.

The Six Covenants:
Essentials to Keep You on the Path

In every creative process, there is a recurring pattern of actions that interweaves faith, love, vision, and integrity. These four acts comprise a matrix, which is the essence of all created things.

Though we have linked creativity and art in our culture, these two are not the only companions. Human beings can be creative in any sphere of life. Consciously or not, we express our creativity in myriad ways. In our everyday lives, we express our creativity when we:

- Cook, garden, court, love, parent, sew, pray, worship, dance, and listen.

In our work alone or with others, we express our creativity when we:

- Plan, design, build, teach, manage, administer, heal, counsel, nurse, minister, and contemplate.

In our times of retreat and renewal, we express our creativity when we:

- Draw, paint, write, sing, meditate, hum, compose, sculpt, exercise, drum, tell stories, and revel in stillness and silence.

Whether we engage in these creative realms for vocation or leisure, each is a reflection of our signature presence. And each calls upon our faith, love, vision, and integrity.

Throughout time and across cultures, faith, love, vision, and integrity consistently connect one creative act to another. These four covenants also connect us to a power beyond ourselves—the grace, benevolence, and might of God.

As I've become more conscious of my own creative process, I've recognized that while the power of faith, love, vision, and integrity are essential, they are not sufficient. Faith, love, vision, and integrity are magnified by the covenants of gratitude and legacy.

Gratitude, the parent of all the covenants, opens our hearts and offers the power of blessing. Legacy is both a means and an end unto itself. Legacy is the very reason for the other covenants. Legacy is all about falling in love with the future, living for the sake of passing on a gift that is only yours to give.

Each of the six covenants on the inspirational path offers a unique promise and blessing. The promise is fulfilled when we make a commitment and act on, or give expression to, a covenant.

- *Legacy* honors our deep concern and caring for others. Legacy opens us to the archetype of the Steward, where we are intentional about creating a positive future for others—in our work, our communities, and our relationships with others. Expressing legacy is a way to consciously create the future. Expressing legacy connects us to our highest aim, which is to be a servant to our creativity and thereby of service to God, to future generations, and to ourselves.

- *Gratitude* is the soul's way of rejoicing, a time-honored way of offering acknowledgement and thanks for who you are, where you are, and for others. Expressing gratitude is a way to remember and acknowledge that each day is a precious gift, a blessing. It is also a way of remembering that someone was here before you, paving the way. In the tradition of my African ⚘ ancestors, our first obligation is to express gratitude to God.

- *Faith* is an unshakable devotion to the unknown: a belief in the unseen, the unformed, in that which has yet to become fully tangible or manifest—a bright new idea, an unborn child, a promising experiment, an arresting image that sparks a new poem, painting, or garden. Expressing faith is one way to be true to your beliefs, yourself, others, and to God.

- *Love*, or passion, provides the fuel to move faith forward. Love compels us to give our heart and voice fully to what we care about. Expressing love is a way of saying to the world *this* is what I treasure. When we are passionate about our creative endeavors, we stoke the fire that author and psychologist Marion Woodman describes as "the creative fire," the fire that requires no fuel.

- *Vision* is the bridge that connects us to the future, for it allows us to hold in our mind's eye, our heart, and our soul images of our passion. Expressing vision is a way of falling in love with the future. We fall in love with the future by envisioning or imagining what we want to create. We express our vision most deeply when we engage our outer as well as our inner ways of seeing and knowing.

- *Integrity* invites us to be our whole selves wherever we are. When we express our integrity, it means we are the same person with our children as with our partners, we are the same at work as at the dry cleaners, grocery store, and church. Expressing our integrity means that we are relentlessly honest with ourselves and others; we do not hide or edit ourselves, we do not pretend to be small. We let our brilliance shine forth.

Why are the six covenants so important on the inspirational path? Each covenant offers us the power of a blessing.

- *Legacy* offers us the power of stewardship. It is this stance toward service that enables us to create and leave a shining future for our children and our children's children.

- *Gratitude* offers us the power of blessing. Blessings open the doors of our heart, which is the wellspring of our creativity, a bridge between God's grace and our future.

- *Faith* offers us the power of unshakable devotion. In faith's embrace, we can proceed boldly even in the midst of chaos and uncertainty.

- *Love* offers us the dual powers of passion and purpose. Love shores up our faith and fuels our creativity.

- *Vision* offers us the power of inner and outward sight. Along with faith and love, vision pulls us across the bridge to imagine and create an irresistible future.

- *Integrity* offers us the power of wholeness and truth. Only when we claim the authority of our own true voice are we invested with the power to heal and transform ourselves and others.

Using This Book

Using *Legacy Living* is like having a trusted friend or ally to support you on the inspirational path. Return to this resource over and over again to remind you to take time to reflect, to develop the necessary habits to honor your creativity, to regard each covenant as a sacred commitment to yourself.

I encourage you to use a journal to help you track your process. Use your journal to take notes, record your thoughts, write, draw pictures. Your journal will become the personal map of your journey.

Legacy Living is organized into six main chapters. Each chapter focuses on one of the six universal covenants that are key to legacy living. I begin each chapter with a poem or excerpt that expresses the essence of the covenant explored in that chapter.

Throughout the book, I include stories, anecdotes, quotes, questions, and pictures to illuminate the covenants and engage your creativity. Savor and enjoy them. I encourage you to add some of your own. Include your hopes, wishes, dreams, and triumphs. I encourage you to make this book and your journal living reflections of who you are. Turn them into your own personal treasure chest. This book and your journal can be resources for you to draw on for many years to come.

It is essential to take each covenant to heart and to begin acting on them by acknowledging and celebrating yourself and what's important to you. As a place to acknowledge and celebrate your blessings, I invite you to create a special place of sanctuary.

Your sanctuary can be simple or elaborate. Your place of sanctuary can be a special chair or table or an

You must have a room, or a certain hour or so a day, where you don't know what was in the newspapers that morning, you don't know who your friends are, you don't know what you owe anybody, you don't know what anybody owes to you. This is a place where you can simply experience and bring forth what you are and what you might be. This is the place of creative incubation.

– Joseph Campbell

area of your living or work space. It can be indoors or outdoors. Create a space that feels right for you. Be gentle with yourself. Start simply. The important thing is that you set aside a special place that is just for you. You are worthy of the time you take to nurture yourself.

Use your sanctuary. It will keep you on your journey, providing a haven for reflection, respite, and celebration. Your sanctuary is a place where you can be free from the regular routine of your everyday life, free of interruptions, a place to nourish and replenish your soul. It is a place to come home to yourself, to get grounded.

Your sanctuary is a refuge for self-renewal and discovery, a welcoming haven for your imagination, providing protective harbor and a point of departure for exploring new regions and dimensions of yourself. Creating and using your sanctuary is a way of saying yes to yourself, your creativity, and to God. Your sanctuary is essential to support your legacy living.

At the end of the book, you'll find a collection of suggested readings and other resources to engage and sustain you along your inspirational path.

Legacy
The Power of Stewardship

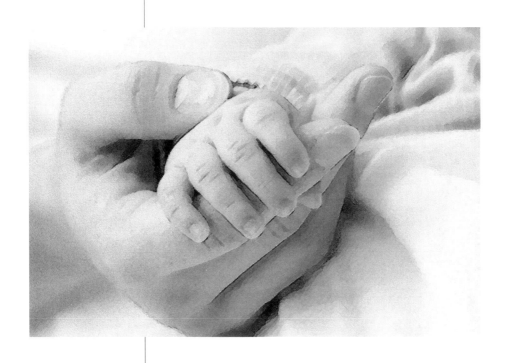

White Lilies

for my mother, Mildred Blackmon McEwen

Standing tall
on that glorious September day.

Indian Summer.
No other sound
save for the cleansing stream—

mourner's tears—

and Cousin Clara's wails
cutting the husky air:
Oh, Jesus! Help me, Jesus!
She hollered for us all.

And there you stood
gathering lilies
life from the grave
seeing beyond the coming storms:
five white stars a blaze of blessings
surrendered from your bosom
a mother's prayer.

– Gloria Burgess

Life's most persistent and urgent question is,
What are you doing for others?

– Dr. Martin Luther King, Jr.

Legacy

The Power of Stewardship

Legacy is about building a bridge to the future. Legacy is about leaving a shining inheritance for our children and our children's children.

We leave a legacy whether we are conscious of it or not. Consistent with the time-honored cultural and spiritual wisdom where legacy is the act of consciously creating something of enduring value, our goal, too, is to be intentional about our legacy.

Because the commitment is to create for the future with intention and foresight, the covenant of legacy focuses on two essential questions: *What do I want to create? And for whom?* To respond to these questions is to act on the knowledge that inside each of us is a glorious world waiting to be born. To help give birth to these magnificent new worlds, we must be midwives for one another.

On the inspirational path, the covenant of legacy both completes and regenerates the creative cycle. As an end unto itself, legacy is our very reason for being. Legacy is why we quest after our own true voice. Legacy is why we aspire to live a creative, authentic life. Legacy is why we bring forth our signature presence.

26

Legacy living calls each one of us to keep our creative fire burning *and* to pass the flame on to others. If we are attentive, we can find inspiration to pass the flame on wherever we are. One place to find inspiration is to look at the legacy of ordinary and extraordinary individuals.

From the time he was a young boy in rural Mississippi, my father dreamed of living in a house with running water and of attending college. For him, getting a "good education" was a ticket to freedom. He'd be able to leave the South and poverty behind. The first in his family to aspire to attend college, my father had few prospects of earning enough money to pay for college himself. Even so, he was committed to his dream.

After many years of holding fast to his dream of attending college, God opened the doors for my father. Although he wasn't able to take classes there, he worked as a janitor at Ol' Miss—the University of Mississippi. My father talked to anyone who would listen about his dream of going to college. When he spoke with one of the professors there, God opened another door, then another.

The professor told the Dean of Ol' Miss about my father, and he told someone else. That someone else was William Faulkner, who became my father's benefactor. Faulkner paid my father's college expenses and ensured that he, my mother, me, and my sisters had clothes to wear. What kind of faith must Faulkner have had to befriend a black man at a time in our nation's history when Jim Crow laws still prevailed? And what kind of black man would be befriended by a white man at a time such as this?

Faulkner and my father were both extraordinary men. Gifted, reclusive, but not reticent, Faulkner's

One can never pay in gratitude. One can only "pay in kind" somewhere else in life.

– Anne Morrow Lindbergh

legacy of providing much-needed financial support, of taking a stand on behalf of a black man directly benefited my father. Befriending my father and becoming his benefactor was Faulkner's way of contributing to dismantling the walls of institutionalized racism long before desegregation was mandated in the South.

My father's legacy was his unflagging determination and his abiding commitment to his dream of going to college. Though my father initially declined Faulkner's generous financial support because he didn't see how he'd be able to repay him, God opened another door. Faulkner said he didn't expect my father to repay him; he simply asked my father to pass a kindness on to someone else along the way.

In myriad ways throughout his life, my father passed his blessing on to others. Most importantly, he passed on his legacy of faith in himself and in the power of holding onto and manifesting his dream.

A dream without action is just a hallucination.

– Anonymous

To honor my father's legacy of unshakable devotion to his dream and Faulkner's legacy of faith in my father to help him achieve his dream, I wrote a poem called *Sanctuary*. An antiphon of courage and faith, *Sanctuary* is a tribute to two men who had the resolve to move against the tide at a time in our history when it was unfashionable for whites to extend a hand to blacks and almost unthinkable for a black man to imagine a life other than the one into which he was born.

Sanctuary

for William Faulkner & Earnest McEwen, Jr.

Between the brush of angels' wings
and furious hooves of hell, two mortal men
fell down. How you must have looked—
white shirt stained, khakis fatigued,
smelling of sweat and smoke,
hair at odds with itself and the world.
At the threshold among your restless dead
in echo and shadow of ancient oaks,
providing sanctuary, offering shade,
you had many worlds behind you,
few yet to be born: stories of insurgence,
scorn, decay—theme and variations
of a vanquished South.

Leaning against a jamb
of antebellum brass, you watched, waited,
raised weary arm and hand, saluted
the familiar stranger. *Come. Enter. Sit. Sing.*

You reached each other across the grate.
What you two must have known of heaven and hell.

Like my father and Faulkner, we are also stewards of the future. We must be willing to stand up for what we know and for what is right, for unless and until we do, we will continue to co-create a world riven by social, spiritual, moral, political, and economic decay. Those whose voices have been repressed, oppressed, and suppressed will continue to be silenced or erased.

As 21st-century stewards, we are called to take a stand, lift our voices, and embrace one another because of and in spite of our differences. For the sake of our children, our only response must be a

For anything worth having one must pay the price; and the price is always work, patience, love, and self-sacrifice.

– John Burroughs

resounding declaration and daily demonstration to be the change we want to see.

Mary Jane Gillespie, my sixth-grade teacher, was not only a fine teacher, she also exemplified legacy living. Lucky for me, she saw behind my brave facade of quiet desperation. I entered her class with a spirit that had become malnourished through benign neglect, ignorance, and outright prejudice.

In Detroit, I lived in multi-racial and multi-ethnic neighborhoods, but my classmates were predominantly black. When I was in the fifth grade my family moved from Detroit, where I excelled in school, to Ann Arbor, Michigan. In Ann Arbor, I was one of only a handful of blacks among a sea of mostly white classmates.

My fifth-grade teacher all but ignored me in the classroom. Day by day, I could feel myself getting smaller, becoming more and more withdrawn. I lived for recess, because it allowed me some freedom to be myself. When the bell rang, I would linger outside until the last possible moment. I hated going back into the dreaded classroom.

By contrast to my fifth-grade experience, in Ms. Gillespie's sixth-grade classroom I felt engaged and alive. Every shelf and ledge held some fascinating book, picture, musical instrument, sculpture, model, or some kind of wonderful gadget. From the ceiling hung our ever-changing display of colorful mobiles. The whole back wall was filled with books of varying levels of reading difficulty.

Ms. Gillespie didn't mind if we borrowed books as long as we brought them back in the same "or better" condition. "Better" simply meant that you read the book you borrowed. Because I completed my class assignments quickly, I often borrowed a book to read while others finished their work. I especially enjoyed reading the books of poetry.

One day Ms. Gillespie suggested I take a look at a small blue book of poems called *The Dream Keeper* by Langston Hughes. This edition had poems and pictures made from woodcuts. As I read the poems, I realized this was the first time I had held a whole book of poems where the language sounded like the language I spoke at home and the people in the woodcuts had eyes and lips that looked like mine.

I read those poems over and over, memorizing many of them, imprinting their familiar, rich rhythms in my heart and on my soul. Langston Hughes' *The Dream Keeper* provided the right medicine to heal my wounded soul. It was the cool refreshing water I needed to restore my withered spirit.

Hughes' legacy in my life was immense. Ms. Gillespie's legacy was immeasurable. Years later, she gave me yet another gift—a hard-bound copy of *The Dream Keeper*, with a lovely note that still makes my heart sing. Wherever you are, Ms. Gillespie, I thank you for your keen insight and wisdom.

The revelation of Ms. Gillespie's legacy is still unfolding in me. And now, when I have an opportunity to share poetry and story and art and song with young people, I tell them the story of a woman who knew the deep meaning of education—*educare*—to draw forth with gratitude, faith, love, vision, and integrity.

I can only imagine whose shoulders Ms. Gillespie stands on. I humbly stand on hers with profound gratitude for her legacy to me and countless others.

Social visionary and innovator Bill Shore writes about the work of legacy in his book *The Cathedral Within*. He describes his desire to do something to

It happens that the work which is likely to be our most durable moment and to convey some knowledge of us to the most remote posterity is a work of bare utility; not a shrine, not a process, not a place, but a bridge.

– Harper's Weekly, 1883

The aspiration to be part of something bigger and more lasting is universal in human nature.

– Bill Shore

make the most of his life, "something that counts," something that makes a difference in the lives of others. For Shore, this means doing something that not only makes a difference, but has a lasting impact.

Shore's pioneering work has resulted in innovative and successful anti-hunger and anti-poverty efforts worldwide, culminating in new ways of thinking about community and mobilizing for the redistribution of wealth. At the heart of Shore's legacy is engaging the leadership of individuals who possess what he calls "the spirit of cathedral builders," those individuals who commit "their life's work to something larger than themselves, to something so large it may be unfinishable" in their life span.

Legacy living calls us to engage our whole self in all our endeavors. We must also remember that we were created to be in relationship. We need one another. More often than not, legacy is co-created. As anthropologist Margaret Mead reminds us, "Never doubt that a small group of thoughtful, committed citizens can change the world. Indeed, it is the only thing that ever has."

At the beginning of this book, I invited you to open yourself to the promise of change. Legacy living is all about change.

Legacy is why we express gratitude for our blessings, give thanks to others, and honor to our ancestors. Legacy is why we are faithful to our vision and take a thousand actions to realize it. Legacy is the reason we express our passion whether it be through our work, to our loved ones, in our communities, or for God. Legacy is why we dive into the depths of who we are, ascend for air and break through the hard surface to reveal the magnificence of who we are, walking in the strength and power of freedom and integrity.

Grass is the forgiveness of nature— her constant benediction... Forests decay, harvests perish, flowers vanish, but grass is immortal.

– John James Ingalls

We are all ready to be savage in some cause. The difference between a good man and a bad one is the choice of the cause.

– William James

I was happy to have children... I wanted my body, as well as my mind and spirit to succeed, to reach an appropriate glory.

– Gwendolyn Brooks

Invitation

If not now, when? If not you, who?

– adapted from Rabbi Hillel

By expressing legacy on behalf of someone or something each day, you nurture its inclusion into your natural way of being. Your daily expression of legacy will soon become a habit, and a habit becomes a part of you.

I invite you to set aside time each day for the next few weeks to respond to one or more of the questions and activities in the next section "Reflections and Discoveries."

To focus on the covenant of legacy, begin by finding or creating a special place in your home, office, or outdoors. This special place is your sanctuary. Your sanctuary is a sacred place, a place of respite and "creative incubation." Your sanctuary can also be a place of refreshment and renewal, a time or place to reflect on what and for whom you are creating a legacy.

There are many ways to make your place of sanctuary special. You might play your favorite music, burn incense, add fresh flowers, or draw inspiration from a photo of a loved one or a favorite quote.

In your place of sanctuary, take a moment to set your intention in this sacred space. I like to light a candle, a time-honored way of bringing light into darkness. Lighting a candle is also a way of honoring precious souls who have crossed over, of focusing our attention on what truly matters.

Do not go where the path may lead. Go instead where there is no path and leave a trail.

– Ralph Waldo Emerson

Remember that finding or creating and spending time in your sanctuary is not a luxury. It is an imperative. It is necessary for nurturing your authentic voice, your creative gifts, your signature presence.

———◇———

Each day, for a week, place an item signifying legacy in your sanctuary—a special candle, photo, letter, flower, poem, prayer, ring, incense, or favorite book.

Each time you add a new object or keepsake, take a moment to say aloud for whom you are creating a legacy. Giving voice to your legacy is a way of em*body*ing it, a way to hold it more deeply in your body's memory.

———◇———

In your journal or in the space below, I invite you to make a covenant with yourself to express legacy on behalf of or for someone or something daily.

Reflections and Discoveries

🍃 What does legacy mean to you? What is the rhythm of legacy in your life?

🍃 Who has guided you, encouraged you, been a beacon of light for you? Whoever they are, they have left a legacy for you. Write their names here.

🍃 Jot down the legacy each person left for you. How did he or she touch your life?

❧ Choose one person and write about how he or she has made a difference in your life. How were you shaped by this person?

❧ What do you want to create as your legacy? For whom—your children, a spouse or partner, a niece or nephew?

❧ How do you think your legacy will make a difference to this person? To others?

❧ "I believe in you." Can you recall a time when someone said or silently expressed those words to you? What effect did these words have on you?

❧ Have you ever said "I believe in you" to someone else? Why? What effect did these words have on the person to whom you said them?

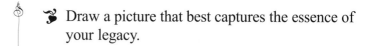 Draw a picture that best captures the essence of your legacy.

❧ Write your favorite quotes as reminders of what it means to leave a legacy.

❧ Create a legacy ribbon. You will need three to four feet of ribbon or twine. Gather a handful of colorful buttons, beads, charms, scraps of cloth, feathers, photos—any small item that has meaning for you. To create your legacy ribbon, focus on the questions below. As you respond to each question, find a button, bead, charm— whatever captures the essence and thread the ribbon through or around it.

- Who named you?

- Were you named for someone in your family? If so, who?

- Where were you born?

- Where did you spend your childhood?

- How did the place where you were born or grew up shape you to become the person you are today?

- What were your favorite childhood memories?

- What were difficult memories from your childhood?

- How did these difficult memories shape you?

- So far, what have been the most joyful times in your life?

- So far, what have been your most significant blessings?

- Describe your most treasured beliefs and values about people.

- Pick five words that you would pass along to a young person that captures your philosophy about life.

🐿 Note the date you create your legacy ribbon. Each year on this date, re-visit your legacy to renew your covenant to yourself. Add to and subtract from it. Each year, take time to reflect on and reassess your covenant. Keeping your covenant up to date will inspire you to reaffirm your commitment to the shining legacy you will leave for others.

Gratitude

The Power of Blessing

Whispers at Dawn

Hush now.
    Listen.
    Lean into those voices
    that whisper at dawn.

Stand gently
    proudly
    on the broad bones
    the great shoulders

of the grand mothers and fathers
    who dreamt you
        and held you
    keep you
        and walk with you
    stroking your face
        as dawn paints
    that canvas of sky.

– Gloria Burgess

*Gratitude is not only the greatest of virtues,
but the parent of all the others.*

– Cicero

Gratitude

The Power of Blessing

*Consciously culti-
vating thankful-
ness is a journey
of the soul, one
that begins when
we look around us
and see the posi-
tive effects that
gratitude creates.*

– M. J. Ryan

Gratitude is the inner recognition and outward acknowledgment of our blessings. We become familiar with the grammar of gratitude in our family by learning to say "thank you" to others for their kindness or generosity, by saying grace before meals, or praying at bedtime. We expand the grammar of gratitude by consciously paying attention to and acknowledging our abundant blessings. And we enrich it by blessing all of creation—other people, our experiences, animals, plants, our hopes and dreams, our memories, and even our fears.

Legacy living calls us to bless both the good and the bad, our opportunities and our challenges, our pleasure and our pain. By doing so, we deepen and strengthen our commitment to gratitude. We also learn that the act of blessing is reciprocal. When we offer blessings, we are blessed, and we widen the circle of being a blessing to others. In this way, blessing not only becomes its own reward, it becomes the very fabric of our lives.

We express gratitude outwardly by acknowledging and proclaiming our blessings either in solitude or in community with others. Recounting our blessings brings forth new life, new possibilities. Just as a rose requires water and soil to grow, human beings require the life-giving waters of gratitude to nurture and sustain us. Each time we acknowledge our blessings, we are granted an opportunity to draw deeply from our source, the wellspring of our creativity. When we acknowledge our blessings, we create joy. Like love, joy multiplies when we give it away.

On the inspirational path, the covenant of gratitude begins and ends with thanks giving. In my own practice of gratitude, I give thanks to God, the infinitude, the source of my inspiration and of our individual and collective creativity. I also give thanks to my earthly father and mother and the procession of elders who preceded them, my ancestors who sacrificed often and dearly to pave the way for their sons and daughters and therefore for me.

By practicing the covenant of gratitude, I pay a debt while making a sacred commitment to God, my ancestors, and myself. When I express the covenant of gratitude, I also acknowledge that I already have access to what I need—an abundant spirit, which is replenished in communion with myself, family and friends, and God. In a lovely contemporary translation, the opening words of the 23rd Psalm remind me of this blessing:

Gratitude is the heart's memory.

– French Proverb

> *The Lord is my shepherd*
> *I have everything I need.*

I am blessed to know that my table is already set and waiting—just for me. All I need to do is feast on and share my blessings.

In addition to God, we have a wealth of others to whom we must be able to express gratitude. By acknowledging and appreciating where and who we come from, we can fully reap the bounty of our inheritance. That inheritance includes the many blessings that come from our real or adopted mothers, fathers, grandparents, aunts, and uncles, who loved us and sacrificed a measure of their lives for our benefit. Our inheritance also includes the place or places we call home, those havens that provide shelter, solace, and sustenance. When we give thanks to God, our relations, and other nurturing presences, we say "no" to isolation. Instead, we open our hearts to belonging, finding our place in community with others. And as our hearts open, we open to the creative magnificence of our own true nature, our authenticity, the source of our own true voice.

When I feel stuck or blocked in my writing, I only have to think about and say *thank you* to the multitude of poets and other writers on whose shoulders I stand. I simply recall a word or a phrase and am flooded with a sense of gratefulness for the generous spirit of a favorite poet or essayist or novelist. In their company, I feel a sense of belonging to the past, present, and future. And I know that I am held in the edifying embrace of women and men who struggled just as I do, just as we all do at one time or another. Because I know that these women and men prevailed and triumphed, I am also encouraged, inspired to press in and press on.

In my public speaking and in my work with organizations, I always begin by giving thanks for someone or something important in my life. Depending on the setting, I invite participants to reflect on two or three people who are no longer living, individuals who contributed or somehow made an impact on their lives. To bring these individuals into conscious awareness, I invite participants to say the names of those they wish to acknowledge, to thank them for their influence and whispering presence.

There is no house like the house of belonging.

– David Whyte

This ritual of acknowledgment—calling the ancestors—is a way of expressing gratitude. Sometimes I include other elements in the ritual, such as pouring a libation. In organizational settings or community gatherings, I invite participants to invoke the ancestors, usually founders or other prominent, memorable individuals. Depending on the context of our work, I ask that their names be written on a piece of paper and that their contribution be acknowledged silently or aloud.

Regardless of the setting, the purposes for calling the ancestors are the same:

- To remember and acknowledge those who came before us.

- To show honor and respect for those who paved the way for us.

- To express our gratitude for their vision and for giving us broad shoulders on which to stand.

- To recount our blessings for their sacrifices so that our life might be less troubled and, hopefully, better than theirs.

- To take our rightful place in the human family and take up our residence in the great house of belonging.

To fully inhabit the house of belonging, to fully inhabit our own lives, we must be consciously connected to where and who we came from. We must claim our ancestral inheritance—the beautiful ones and the not-so beautiful ones. To do so is to take necessary steps in our journey toward wholeness— toward our integration and integrity.

Creating a Ritual of Acknowledgment

When pouring a libation, I use plain tap water, although you can also use other liquids. In workshop settings, I might add pebbles, pieces of colored glass, rose petals, rosemary, or lavender buds to fully engage the senses and to signify a specific intention, focusing on remembrance, blessing, healing, beauty, love—whatever infuses the occasion with meaning.

51

Even if we feel disconnected from them or because of difficult circumstances we do not hold our ancestors in high esteem, we owe them our respect. *Respect*, from the Latin *respicio*, means to look again. When we take the time to look again, we can acknowledge the past, whether it was painful or pleasurable. We can acknowledge our ancestors for whatever part they played in shaping us into who we are. We can look at whatever imprints they might have left on our lives, take stock of their legacy, and make conscious choices about our own lives. We can then take full responsibility for our own legacies, which are always in the making.

A number of years ago I fell in love with a sculpture called *The Grandmothers*. Though I no longer remember the artist's name, I recall that I was struck by this life-sized testament and tribute of thanksgiving to my ancestors. The sculpture tells an intergenerational story that spans two continents and four hundred years, the story—familiar and unique—of four women of African descent.

When I first saw *The Grandmothers*, I read the sculpture's story from the bottom to the top. On the bottom, a barefoot, ebony-hued woman assumes a squatting posture; she is arrayed in brightly colored *kente* cloth, draped to cover her body and wrapped around her head as a headdress. Her shoulders support a chocolate-skinned woman with straight knees and bent back. This somber-faced, high-cheeked woman wears a sweat-stained head rag and a long, gray full-skirted dress of a slave. On her tattered apron is a small patch of the brightly colored *kente* cloth passed on to her from her foremother.

On the slave woman's shoulders stands an arresting yet weary-eyed woman dressed in a 1920s style red chemise. This bronze-faced woman wears matching red shoes and several long, beaded necklaces. She sports a red purse and in her right hand holds a long red plume. Inside her open purse is a small handkerchief made from the apron passed on to her by her foremother. Standing on her shoulders at the top of *The Grandmothers* is a bright-eyed, straight-backed woman, dressed in a contemporary tailored suit. Her skin is the color of saffron. On her white jacket, above her heart, she wears a stunning pin made of crystal and gold, set against a feathery backdrop of red made from the plume passed on to her by her foremother.

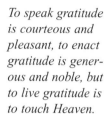

To speak gratitude is courteous and pleasant, to enact gratitude is generous and noble, but to live gratitude is to touch Heaven.

– Johannes A. Gaertner

When I reflect on *The Grandmothers*, I appreciate it as a stunning sculpture and as an offering of profound gratitude. The African and African-American women in this remarkable sculpture pay homage not only to the generations of women who came before us, they also point the way to possibility, inviting us to imagine future generations who will learn from, embrace, and stand upon the supporting shoulders of one another.

Just as *The Grandmothers* enables us to glimpse into the past and the future, composer and singer Ysaye Barnwell reminds us in her beautiful and uplifting song, *We Are...*, that each one of us holds a stake in the past and the future, for each of us is the embodiment of a sacred dream. Each one of us embodies and carries forth the dream of our ancestors—our foremothers and forefathers who broke new ground, paved the way, birthed new songs, envisioned new worlds and new landscapes vastly different from their own.

We Are...

For each child that's born
a morning star rises
and sings to the universe
who we are.

We are our grandmothers' prayers.
We are our grandfathers' dreamings.
We are the breath of our ancestors.
We are the spirit of God.

We are
Mothers of courage
Fathers of time
Daughters of dust
Sons of great vision.

We are
Sisters of mercy
Brothers of love
Lovers of life and
the builders of nations.

We are
Seekers of truth
Keepers of faith
Makers of peace and
the wisdom of ages.

Thank you for being.

– Seneca Greeting

If you read the words of this song silently, read them again—aloud. As you do, listen to the rhythm and cadence of the words. As you say the words, move to their rhythms. Notice what happens in your body. Can you visualize the images that Barnwell paints with the words? On a sheet of paper or in your journal, draw a picture of what you see.

All of these activities—reading in silence, reading aloud, moving, visualizing, and drawing—invite us to pay attention, to witness, and to experience the sacred. They invite us to cross a threshold to leave *chronos* time, or clock time, and enter into *kairos* time, that place where for a blessed few hours clock time stands still, ceasing to exist.

Kairos, also known as God's time, invites us into moments of eternity. Entering *kairos* is a way of integrating the sacred in our lives and is a time-honored way of expressing gratitude. We enter *kairos* in many ways, including writing and reading poetry, creating and listening to stories, singing, dancing, running, gardening, cooking, meditating, worshiping, spending time in nature, and spending time in solitude. Each of these modes of expression invites the sacred into our everyday lives.

The sacred is also profoundly manifest in ceremony, ritual, praise, and prayer. Through these gates we enter into and become one with God. Through these gates we glimpse eternity. Through these gates we experience holiness and wholeness.

When we experience wholeness, our own true voice resonates within and outwardly. We come into a rhythm that ethnomusicologist Eva Jessye calls "first nature," the rhythm of being in tune with our life's purpose or calling. For Irish poet and theological scholar John O'Donohue, first nature is when we come into rhythm with our life. "When you are in rhythm with your nature, nothing destructive can touch you. Providence is at one with you; it minds you and brings you to your new horizons."

By acting on the covenant of gratitude—weaving thankfulness, acknowledgment, and blessings

Kairos is ontological. In Kairos time, we are fully in isness... fully, wholly, positively.

– Madeleine L'Engle

We need to into the daily cadence of our lives—we take the nec-

We need to 𝄞 into the daily cadence of our lives—we take the nec-
remember the essary first steps of getting into rhythm with our-
inner music selves, into the very essence of who we are. We
that holds us forge a partnership with Providence to imagine new
every moment horizons, to give birth to new worlds.
in such a
strong rhythm
of belonging.   To deepen your understanding and appreciation
    for how you might express gratitude, I invite you to
– John O'Donohue take time to reflect on and discover its many facets.
Begin by reviewing the following sections:
"Invitation" and "Reflections and Discoveries."
Notice what you're drawn to and what you resist. In
this sovereign journey of the soul, remember to be
gracious and gentle with yourself.

Invitation

If not now, when? If not you, who?

– adapted from Rabbi Hillel

By expressing gratitude for someone or something each day, you nurture its inclusion into your natural way of being. Your daily expression of gratitude will soon become a habit, and a habit becomes a part of you.

I invite you to set aside time each day for the next few weeks to respond to one or more of the questions and activities in the next section "Reflections and Discoveries."

To focus on the covenant of gratitude, begin by finding or creating a special place in your home, office, or outdoors. This special place is your sanctuary. Your sanctuary is a sacred place, a place of respite and "creative incubation." Your sanctuary can also be a place of refreshment and renewal, a time or place to shower yourself with gratitude, a place to give thanks and take note of your many blessings.

There are many ways to make your place of sanctuary special. You might play your favorite music, burn incense, add fresh flowers, or draw inspiration from a photo of a loved one or a favorite quote.

In your place of sanctuary, take a moment to set your intention in this sacred space. I like to light a candle, a time-honored way of bringing light into darkness. Lighting a candle is also a way of honor-

ing precious souls who have crossed over, of focusing our attention on what truly matters.

Remember that finding or creating and spending time in your sanctuary is not a luxury. It is an imperative. It is necessary for nurturing your authentic voice, your creative gifts, your signature presence.

———◈———

Each day, for a week, place an item signifying gratitude in your sanctuary—a special candle, photo, letter, flower, poem, prayer, ring, incense, or favorite book.

There are only two ways to live your life. One is as though nothing is a miracle. The other is as if everything is.

– Albert Einstein

Each time you add a new object or keepsake, take a moment to say aloud what you are grateful for, what blessing it has offered to you. Giving voice to your blessings is a way of em*body*ing the blessing, a way to hold it more deeply in your body's memory.

———◈———

In your journal or in the space below, I invite you to make a covenant with yourself to express gratitude to or for someone or something daily.

Reflections and Discoveries

🐾 What does gratitude mean to you? What is the rhythm of gratitude in your life?

🐾 In what ways do you express gratitude in your life?

🐾 Jot down the names of three people to whom you are thankful for being in your life. For each person, jot down why you are grateful to him or her.

-

-

-

Write each person a note of thanks and mail it this week.

Take a gratitude walk. As you walk, reflect on and count your blessings. On your return, reflect on the ways you have been a blessing to others.

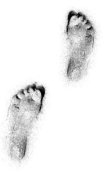

 Who is your favorite relative? What are some of his or her special qualities? Have you expressed thanks to him or her for being in your life?

❧ Find a memorable photo of a favorite relative who is no longer living. Tape or glue the photo in the space below.

❧ Why did you choose this person? Use the margin to jot down your relative's favorite food, color, and saying. If you're not sure, use your imagination, given what you know about her or him.

❧ Give the photo a name. Write it beneath the photo.

🐾 For what do you wish to thank her or him?

Attentiveness is all; I sometimes think of prayer as a certain quality of attention that comes upon me when I'm doing something else.

– Kathleen Norris

🐾 How is she or he connected to your creativity?

🐾 In the space below or in your journal, write a few sentences or a short poem of thanks to your relative.

🐦 In what ways do you express gratitude through ceremony, ritual, movement, song, praise, or prayer? Which are your favorites and why?

🐦 Jot a note here or in your journal, describing your favorite ceremony, ritual, movement, song, praise, or prayer. What stands out for you (e.g., location, colors, textures, aromas, season)? As a reminder, tape or glue magazine clippings, photos, or drawings in the space below.

If we live long enough and deep enough and authentically enough, gratitude becomes a way of life.

– Mark Nepo

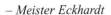

If the only prayer you ever say in life is "thank you" it will be enough.

– Meister Eckhardt

If you do not include ceremony, ritual, movement, song, praise, and prayer in your life, jot a note to yourself about how might you begin to include them. One way to begin is by saying a word or phrase of gratitude—*thank you for this moment*—and repeat it every day for 40 days.

Faith

The Power of Unshakable Devotion

Psalm for Skylar

Before she knew him
    she saw him fly.
No one believed her but
    she felt him grow wings
and with a mother's heart
    she found his name
already written on high.

Driving that day
miles from home
with the eyes of heaven
her mother saw rivers of blood.

The rest is hard.

Like mother
like daughter
she carries on.

The assurance was all
in the doctor's smile.

Never mind
her body's dead weight.

Three thousand days. Still
she counts, finds solace, gives praise
    she *saw* him fly
into the fold of her Father's hands.

– Gloria Burgess

Faith

The Power of Unshakable Devotion

Faith is the abiding belief in someone or something that has yet to become fully tangible or manifest. The fragile beginnings of a new friendship, an untested idea—both find hospitality in faith's harbor and take shape within its protective shelter. Faith asks us to wait, to dwell in a state of unknowing, to hold the necessary tension between current reality and what we envision, in what has yet to be outwardly seen. Paradoxically, faith also beckons us to leave that state of suspended unknowing. For if our creative vision is to be realized, we must venture beyond the ledge and take our own leap of faith into the mystery.

On the inspirational path, the covenant of faith has four facets, each as necessary as air—*faith in yourself, faith in your own work, faith outside of yourself,* and *faith beyond your work.*

1. *Faith in yourself* so you can do your best work and be your best self in any setting. To triumph over the would-be saboteurs of self-doubt, negative judgments, and voices of insufficiency, faith in yourself is essential. A monumental gift, faith in yourself unlocks the door of any self-imposed prison and lets your imagination soar.

2. *Faith in your own work,* whether or not your work involves earning a wage, because your work can come only through you. Faith in yourself and your work is that unswerving fidelity to your own uniqueness. As dance pioneer Martha Graham reminds us:

There is a vitality, a life force, a quickening that is translated through you into action, and because there is only one of you in all time, the expression is unique. And if you block it, it will never exist in any other medium. It will be lost. The world will not have it. It is not your business to determine how good it is; not how valuable it is; not how it compares with other expressions. It is your business to keep it yours clearly and directly, to keep the channel open.

If you suppress or hide your creative gifts, you miss out and so do others. Our responsibility is to let God's light shine through us and to be a light for others.

3. *Faith outside of yourself* means that your creativity is dependent on a higher source. Faith outside of yourself connects you to the benevolence, power, and infinitude of God. When I follow my own desires, I can go astray. When I surrender my desires to God I can stay connected to my highest calling.

As a teacher and public speaker, before I begin a workshop or address an audience, I invoke the covenant of faith. Like Moses in the desert, through a simple prayer or invocation, I invite God's life-giving presence to precede me:

> Dear Lord, hold me
> In Your loving embrace.
> Hold me, once again,
> In the palm of Your hand
> And let Your light shine through me.

Somewhere deep within us, we know that true security is not the absence of danger but the presence of faith—faith in ourselves and in our ability to survive.

– Denise Bissonnette

Go before me.
Stand beside me.
Move through me.

By inviting God's presence to go before me, I become more conscious of the privilege afforded me as well as my immense responsibility as I stand in front of an audience. It also reminds me that I am a vessel not for my own agenda but for God's. If I utter this or a similar invocation as I begin each day, how might my day be infused with grace?

4. *Faith beyond your work,* for when you faithfully express your creativity in service to others, you connect to the covenant of legacy, the gift of stewardship and service. Shirley Chisholm, politician and social steward, reminds us that "service is the rent we pay for being on this earth."

Faith is knowing within yourself that a possibility can become a reality.

– Byllye Avery

As stewards of the future, our rent of service is the most important payment we'll make on behalf of our children. Marian Wright Edelman, who has devoted her life's work to lifting up children and advocating for their rights, urges us to take a stand for our children, for they will inherit our legacy:

> Whoever you are, wherever you are anywhere in America, stand up and commit to leave no child behind. If you cannot stand, raise your hands. If you cannot raise your hands, then lift your eyes or open your ears and hearts. If you do, you, our children, and this great nation will do God proud when He comes.

As stewards who live in a global community, our challenge is to respond to its complexities and challenges by extending ourselves not only to children anywhere in America, but to children throughout the world.

A friend who is a master gardener recently gave me a couple of plants from her garden, cuttings from her lilac bush and a clump of what looked like Marguerite daisies. She'd rooted both cuttings in a potting medium other than soil. The lilac seemed sturdy, but the daisies had begun to sag even before she presented them to me. Concerned about their imminent demise, I signaled my wariness to my friend. With her usual exuberance, she assured me that the daisies would be fine. "Oh, don't worry," she said. "They'll come right back. They're just like black people." Resilient, I thought, and full of faith.

For several weeks, I faithfully watered the lilac and the daisies. Because it was too hot to risk transplanting them, I kept them in their pots. Day after day, I watched as the daisies descended closer and closer to the ground. Though the green stems sagged, their almost blossoming heads too dehydrated to be revived, I kept watering. The echo of my friend's voice stayed with me, "Don't worry…they're just like black people." After several weeks, my faithful watering was rewarded with tender shoots, the new and barely open leaves emerging from the dark moist bark.

What manner of faith does it take to nurture almost lifeless flowers until they regenerate into something new, fresh, and full of promise? How might this kind of faith sustain me in other areas of my life? What lessons of faith can I take with me no matter where I am?

- Believe what I know to be true, rather than what I see with my eyes.

The poet within won't hold you to your failures; she doesn't define you that way. She wants what comes next and has implicit faith that something will.

– Patrice Vecchione

71

- Attention is nearly everything. The *quality* of my attention *is* everything.

- When one plant dies, another is born, or when one door closes, another one opens.

- Faith, water, light, and the ground beneath my feet are all I really need. All of these provisions are already mine.

- Death, like life, is a transient state. It is an end as well as a beginning.

- God really is in the details.

On the inspirational path, we need the kind of faith that Thomas Moore describes. Moore, a former monk with a background in philosophy, musicology, and psychology, encourages us to regard faith as consisting "more in love than knowledge," a faith that is infused with certain aspects of soul.

In *The Soul's Religion*, Moore writes "faith that has any soul in it will have familiar qualities of soul: change, failure, developments, regressions." By contrast, faith that is more attuned with knowledge, or the kingdoms of the mind, insists on rationality, certainty, explanation. All too easily, this kind of faith can become rigid, hollow, and of no use. Having this kind of faith is, in fact, having no faith at all.

Instinctively, we know by the unplanned turns and detours whether or not our faith is charged with soul—the dough that fills the kitchen with a yeasty aroma but remains an unyielding mass that will not rise, an easy friendship that becomes unexpectedly labored and tense, poems that require countless revisions. As troublesome as these encounters may be, I prefer the soulfulness of their challenge to the steely faith that favors the known and the knowable, the certainty we associate with things tangible and concrete, with what we can explain. At the end of the day, this kind of faith *is* of little use.

Faith imbued with soul entices us to open ourselves to uncertainty. Whether we do so with mild trembling or utter terror, we must yield to what we cannot claim or know with complete certainty.

To act on the covenant of faith, begin with something simple, something routine. If you believe that with each new day, you will wake up, that belief is an act of faith. *Every* beginning—waking up to a new day, the first word on a blank page or screen, a seed sown in the awakening soil of early spring, a touch from a loved one when you've reached a breaking point—each is an act of faith. Walking—placing one foot in front of the other again and again—is an act of faith. Walking step by step through the pages of this book is also a manifestation of faith.

As a poet, when I feel the stirrings of a new poem and begin to write, I summon my belief in the power of experience, memory, and language. I believe that experience, memory, and language are a means of transportation, with the power to move me from one place to another. I simply have to begin, faithfully putting one word after another, over and over again, until I arrive some place other than where I began.

Expressing faith is an act of openness, one of being utterly vulnerable to yourself. Even when you're out of rhythm, lose your bearings, and feel no faith at all, if you are vulnerable to the truth of your experience and let that truth flow through you, you open yourself to

Being faithful is more important than being successful. If we are successful in the world's eyes but unfaithful in terms of what we believe, then we fail others.

– Max DePree

discovery even as you are pulled into the cold dark current. Unknowing yet open, we fall into uncharted waters and into the fullness of ourselves.

David Whyte's poem "Faith" offers us a portrait in miniature of devotion spacious enough to embrace the deep freeze of unbelief and the ember of prayer in anticipation of faith's restorative thaw.

Faith

I want to write about faith
    about the way the moon rises
        over cold snow, night after night,

faithful even as it fades from fullness,
    slowly becoming that last curving and impossible
        sliver of light before the final darkness.

But I have no faith myself
    I refuse it the smallest entry.

Let this then, my small poem,
    like a new moon, slender and barely open,
        be the first prayer that opens me to faith.

Like faith, the poem's first eight lines are stark, simple, insistent, and true. And in the poem's three closing lines, faith—though distant and improbable at the poem's beginning—paradoxically becomes a possibility yet again.

Though we are fickle, changing, and given to faithlessness, we must not dwell there. Like the moon, faith is constant. To be in a covenant relationship with faith, we too, must be constant.

Legacy living calls us to constancy. We must have an abiding devotion to our creativity, certain that our faith, if it serves us well, will be tempered with doubt, failure, setbacks—the qualities that are, at once, disturbing and infused with soul. In these soulful moments, we must also remember that we are constantly supported by divine power.

God is magnanimous, always with us, holding us in a wide embrace. Though we might in our faith-lessness believe that God is dispensable to us, we are not dispensable to God. Whether we call on God or not, God calls to us, delivering sweet missives to our soul, speaking to us through the still small voice within.

How has God been speaking to you lately? When God speaks to you, how do you respond? If you knew you had a terminal illness, would you respond differently? We all have a terminal illness—it's called life. If not now, when? If not you, who?

When my faith wavers, I gather strength from God and the abiding faith of my elders, who with-stood the cruelty and injustice of slavery and passed on its intergenerational inheritance.

By acting on the covenant of faith, we not only nourish ourselves and feed our creativity, we also move a step closer to bringing our dreams into fruition and we draw closer to our own divinity and our partnership with God.

Invitation

If not now, when? If not you, who?

– adapted from Rabbi Hillel

Prayer is not doing, but being. It is not words but the beyond-words experience of coming into the presence of something much greater than oneself.

– Kathleen Norris

By expressing faith in someone or something each day, you nurture its inclusion into your natural way of being. Your daily expression of faith will soon become a habit, and a habit becomes a part of you.

I invite you to set aside time each day for the next month to respond to one or more of the questions and activities in the next section "Reflections and Discoveries."

To focus on the covenant of faith, I invite you to begin by finding or creating a special place in your home, office, or outdoors. This special place is your sanctuary. Your sanctuary is a sacred place, a place of respite and "creative incubation." Your sanctuary can also be a place to acknowledge or restore your faith, a place to honor your awakening or your devotion to seeing not only with the outer eye, but with the inner eye of your heart.

There are many ways to make your place of sanctuary special. You might play your favorite music, burn incense, add fresh flowers, or draw inspiration from a photo of a loved one or a favorite quote.

In your place of sanctuary, take a moment to set your intention in this sacred space. I like to light a candle, a time-honored way of bringing light into darkness. Lighting a candle is also a way of honoring precious souls who have crossed over, of focus-

ing our attention on what truly matters.

Remember that finding or creating and spending time in your sanctuary is not a luxury. It is an imperative. It is necessary for nurturing your authentic voice, your creative gifts, your signature presence.

Each day, for a week, place an item signifying faith in your sanctuary—a special candle, photo, letter, flower, poem, prayer, ring, incense, or favorite book.

Each time you add a new object or keepsake, take a moment to express an aspect of your faith or what your faith has offered to you. Giving voice to your faith is a way of em*body*ing it, a way to hold it more deeply in your body's memory.

A little knowledge that acts is worth infinitely more than much knowledge that is idle.

– Kahlil Gibran

In your journal or in the space below, make a covenant with yourself to express faith in or to someone or something daily.

Reflections and Discoveries

🎵 What does faith mean to you? What is the rhythm of faith in your life?

🎵 In what ways are you faithful to yourself? To your creativity?

🎵 How do you feel when you are faithful to yourself? To your creativity? What color(s) captures your feeling?

In what ways might you celebrate your faith-fulness?

In what ways are you unfaithful to yourself? To your creativity?

How do you feel when you are unfaithful to yourself? To your creativity? What color(s) captures your feelings?

In what ways are you faithless? Is this different than being unfaithful?

Who or what do you fear most at this point in your life? Is there a connection between your fear and your faith?

🐦 Read this excerpt from William Faulkner's acceptance speech for the Nobel Prize.*

> I decline to accept the end of man...I refuse to accept this. I believe that man will not merely endure: he will prevail. He is immortal, not because he alone among creatures has an inexhaustible voice, but because he has a soul, a spirit capable of compassion and sacrifice and endurance. The poet's, the writer's, duty is to write about these things. It is his privilege to help man endure by lifting his heart, by reminding him of the courage and honor and hope and pride and compassion and pity and sacrifice which have been the glory of his past. The poet's voice need not merely be the record of man, it can be one of the props, the pillars to help him endure and prevail.

* You can read his entire acceptance speech at *www.faulkner.com*

Jot down your thoughts about Faulkner's words.

❧ Fill this page with your or others' celebration of faith. Include notes, photos, mementos, quotes, poems, stories.

Love

The Power of Passion

Art Forms

Let the beauty we love be what we do.

$\qquad\qquad$ – Rumi

A dancer dances
not because he cannot write
but because his poems
all torso and thighs
expand and contract
now faster now slower
than he can pen the words
joy longing light loss.

A potter pots
not because she cannot sing
but because turn by turn
she composes her music
from water and ash
with palms that trust and see.

A writer writes
not because she cannot dance
but because her silky glide her
stomp and funga
compel her
to move
swirl thrust bend sway
in rhythms
and patterns
in quiet retreat
in quiet
retreat
in quiet quiet
quiet
retreat.

$\qquad\qquad$ – *Gloria Burgess*

Love

The Power of Passion

Love and creativity are as one. In both, we experience what Picasso describes as being seized by encounter. Love and creativity are portals to the highest and deepest expressions of our own first nature, our authentic selves.

Legacy living calls us to love deeply and passionately. When we truly love who we are and what we do, our heart opens wide, our soul expands, and our spirit soars. We become a sacred vessel, allowing God's light to pour in and shine through us. Then anything is possible.

On the inspirational path, the covenant of love keeps us purposefully connected to our dreams. Love also draws us toward wholeness, in our relationships with others and in the deepest of relationships—the love song we are destined to intone when we join in ecstatic union with our true selves.

On the inspirational path, we're embraced by the many arms of love: *self-love, love for others*, and *divine love. Self-love* is the highest divinity and connects us to the divinity of God. We express self-love when we prize and care for ourselves and when we set, attain, and celebrate our goals. We express self-love when we live with purpose, set appropriate limits and boundaries, and are involved in meaningful relationships with others. We express self-love when we say *yes* and follow through on our commitments. We express self-love when we acknowledge our own inward and outward beauty. We express self-love when we take action that moves us closer to fulfilling our dreams.

Love for others includes other people, living things, experiences, ideas, and so on. We express love for others in many ways:

- In our friendships and in our family.

- In our commitment to a spouse.

- In giving birth to and raising children.

- In collegial relationships with co-workers, mentors, or teachers.

- In our sensual and sexual desires.

- In our encounters with the natural world.

- In our deep attraction to certain colors and textures.

- In our zealous grappling with new ideas.

- In our intense excitement for the new and innovative.

- In our regard for the welfare of others.

- In our unconditional compassion and caring for others, caring that transcends familiarity. This special kind of love for others is called *agape* love.

Divine love is our openness to awe and mystery. Divine love is our love for God, expressed in our wonder, awe, and love of the sacred. It is the quality of love that goes beyond the cognitive, emotional, and physical realms. Divine love is experienced as a

Don't resist life passing through you, because that is God passing through you.

– Don Miguel Ruiz

deep encounter, a deep union with God. As expressed by Saint Paul in his letter to the Corinthians, divine love calls us to "a more excellent way."

> If I speak in the tongues of men and angels, but have not love, I am a noisy gong or a clanging cymbal. And if I have prophetic powers, and understand all mysteries and all knowledge, and if I have all faith, so as to remove mountains, but have not love, I am nothing…[Love] bears all things, believes all things, hopes all things, endures all things. Love never ends.
>
> – I Corinthians 13:1-2; 7-8

Legacy living calls us to self love, love for others, and divine love—even under difficult circumstances. As a young girl growing up in Mississippi and Michigan, I routinely experienced racial discrimination. Even so, I was shocked and deeply wounded when someone who attended our church, which had an all-white membership before we joined, attacked my family. Not with stones but with words. A few years ago, I asked my mother how she tolerated being a member of a church where our family was not welcome. She looked at me with great love in her eyes and said, "No matter how unkind others may be toward us, our responsibility is to love them until they love us back."

One of the most profound expressions of our love is our willingness to live authentically. Living with authenticity requires vulnerability. We must be open to our profound mystery as human beings and to our own particular mystery as well. This requires us to be

There are a hundred and one ways to kneel and kiss the ground.

– Jalal-al-Din-Rumi

In Iraq, a book never had one owner—it had ten. Lucky books, to be held often and gently, by so many hands.

– Naomi Shihab Nye

We live in hope because we believe, like St. Paul, that love never dies.

– Adolfo Pérez Esquivel

available to hear and respond to the voice within, the voice, which is sometimes soft and subtle and at other times loud and fierce, the voice of our soul.

In *Care of the Soul*, Thomas Moore invites us to become poet-curators, or imaginative caretakers, to love and care for our very souls in ways that are particular to who we are. In our contemporary culture, our inclination is to manage our lives as if we're projects or programs instead of persons; with this stance, we view life as something we can control.

Moore invites us to re-imagine our lives not as problems to be solved but as adventures into the extraordinary. Rather than doing everything in our power to wield control, he suggests another way: "to bow down in ignorance and confess our limitations." To bow down in this way calls us to act with compassion for ourselves and to invite God's grace into our lives.

For each of us, an adventure into the extraordinary is a commitment to live life not half-heartedly as we so often do, but to live it whole-heartedly. To live life whole-heartedly is an adventure into the heart of our own creativity, for it is there that we experience our own radiance and touch the center of our majesty.

Legacy living calls us continually to express some form of love. With each new encounter, we must answer this call anew. On the inspirational path, the way of love allows us to embrace our calling, to listen and respond fully to the voice within.

Sources that ignite, renew, and nurture our passion are all around us. These sources include people, places, objects, events, and doing what we love.

People we admire or who inspire us can be catalysts for us. In our culture, these catalysts include

When you begin something, forces outside yourself align and support your endeavor. Writers give themselves to this practice. This is a form of love.

– Patrice Vecchione

spiritual, political, entertainment and media leaders, as well as ordinary people:

- **Mother Teresa.** A catalyst who inspired by her compassionate heart. Mother Teresa reminded us that empathy and caring for others is a worthy calling.

- **Nelson Mandela.** A catalyst who, in the changing winds of the political arena or the stale air of imprisoned isolation, ignites the fire of unflagging devotion to his country and his principles. As elder statesman, Mandela kindles the flames of mercy and grace.

- **Judith Jamison.** In today's embattled arts environment, Jamison blends her business acumen and passion for dance as catalyst of the renowned Alvin Ailey Dance Company.

- **Cirque de Soleil.** This constellation of virtuoso acrobats, jugglers, musicians, dancers, actors, and clowns invoke the archetype of the Magician. Seduced by their brilliance, we fall in love with these catalysts who invite us into the realm of enchantment, allure, wonder, magic, and revelry.

- **A neighbor, friend, or family member.** When we are aware and open to their influence, we find a catalyst in any person under any circumstance.

  ◦ A neighbor who bakes you a loaf of bread or drops by with a fresh batch of cookies to lift your spirits.

  ◦ A friend who divides and digs up the hosta plant you admire to share her bounty with you!

- A sister or brother who calls with just the right word to encourage you when you're feeling down or blue.

All of these acts of love provide precious fuel for us.

Whether they are close by or far away, outdoor or indoor places can be powerful sources to nourish and renew your passion and creativity. These can be places in nature:

- A special garden retreat or sanctuary where your favorite flowers and plants surround you.

- A favorite beach where you enjoy swimming, beachcombing, or watching sunsets or storms.

- The Grand Canyon in Arizona.

- Mount Everest in Nepal.

- Ayers Rock in Australia.

- The giant redwood and sequoia groves in Northern California.

They can be indoor or outdoor places that you or someone else create:

- A comfortable nook furnished with your favorite chair and books.

- The quiet solitude of a chapel, prayer room, or temple.

- A bathtub filled with warm water, surrounded by candles and freshly cut flowers.

- The kitchen table where family and friends gather to share a simple, delicious meal.

God could not be everywhere, so he created mothers.

– Eastern European Proverb

The eye that sees nobility and beauty in what another would regard as ordinary is the eye of prayer.

– Wendy Beckett

Often we find that small objects—notes, photos, keepsakes, mementos—offer insight and inspiration even after the original reason for holding onto them fades. What objects hold hidden treasure for you?

- Letters from your first love?

- A photo of a favorite sister or brother, aunt or uncle?

- A shard of glass bathed and tumbled by the sea picked up years ago at your favorite beach?

- A dried bouquet of flowers celebrating a special birthday or anniversary?

- A childhood teddy bear with matted fur and one eye missing?

People, places, and objects evoke memories of past events or experiences, offer reminders of what we treasure, call to us from a distance. Sometimes a smell or a touch can evoke powerful memories, transporting us back in time.

Beauty assists the soul in its own peculiar way of being.

– Thomas Moore

If love is seated in the heart, it is surely grounded and refined by the soul. For we come to know ourselves and those we love not only in the ecstatic presences of love—joy, elation, desire, sensual and sexual lust and pleasure—but also in its sorrowful mercies as well. In the trough of sorrow's valley, we come to know that longing harrows the heart even as it aerates the soul. In these depths, love's betrayal, disturbances, excesses, or scarcity burnish us. Some of our most rewarding creative ventures and discoveries have their genesis beneath the surface of love's troubling waters.

Sorrow is to the soul what the worm is to the wood.

– Swedish Proverb

Whether fueled by joy or sorrow, when we draw from love's deep well, we tap into the reservoir of our unique genius.

Invitation

If not now, when? If not you, who?

– adapted from Rabbi Hillel

By expressing love for someone or something each day, you nurture its inclusion into your natural way of being. Your daily expression of love will soon become a habit, and a habit becomes a part of you.

I invite you to set aside time each day for the next few weeks to respond to one or more of the questions and activities in the next section "Reflections and Discoveries."

To focus on the covenant of love, begin by finding or creating a special place in your home, office, or outdoors. This special place is your sanctuary. Your sanctuary is a sacred place, a place of respite and "creative incubation." Your sanctuary can also be a place to say aloud what aspect of love is most present for you.

There are many ways to make your place of sanctuary special. You might play your favorite music, burn incense, add fresh flowers, or draw inspiration from a photo of a loved one or a favorite quote.

In your place of sanctuary, take a moment to set your intention in this sacred space. I like to light a candle, a time-honored way of bringing light into darkness. Lighting a candle is also a way of honoring precious souls who have crossed over, of focusing our attention on what truly matters.

Remember that finding or creating and spending time in your sanctuary is not a luxury. It is an imperative. It is necessary for nurturing your authentic voice, your creative gifts, your signature presence.

———◈———

Each day, for a week, place an item signifying love in your sanctuary—a special candle, photo, letter, flower, poem, prayer, ring, incense, or favorite book.

Each time you add a new object or keepsake, take a moment to express your love for someone that has offered love to you. Giving voice to your love is a way of em*body*ing it, a way to hold it more deeply in your body's memory.

———◈———

In your journal or in the space below, I invite you to make a covenant with yourself to express love to or for someone or something daily.

Reflections and Discoveries

❧ What does love mean to you? What is the rhythm of love in your life?

❧ Who do you love? In what ways do you express your love toward him or her?

❧ Who loves you? How do these individuals demonstrate their love for you?

❧ In what ways do you express love for yourself?

❧ Write a love letter to yourself. Create a pretty envelope. Paste it here or in your journal.

❧ What's your favorite color? Where does this color show up for you in your life?

❧ If you could do or be only what you loved for a year, what would you do or be? What's stopping you?

❧ List three things you *love* to do:

1.

2.

3.

❧ Circle your favorite passion. Recall a time when you were so engaged in this passion that you lost all track of time. Make a note of it and remember this passion. When you're distracted or feeling disheartened, you can "come home" by way of this passion.

We are the ones
We are the ones
We've been
   waiting for

– June Jordan

❧ If your daughter or son were looking through your keepsakes after your death, what kind of legacy would they find—one of passion or one of self-betrayal?

🎵 In what ways do you include poetry, stories, singing, and dancing in your life?

🎵 What poems, stories, songs, and dances have you created?

🎵 What poems, songs, and stories do you know by heart?

🎵 What songs do you hum or sing while walking, driving, or taking a shower?

🎵 What dances do you enjoy?

🎵 Do you enjoy dancing with a partner, or dancing alone?

Draw a picture of yourself dancing a dance of appreciation. Color the picture, using your favorite colors.

Let your love be like the misty rain, coming softly, but flooding the river.

– African Proverb

Joy is a net of love by which you can catch souls. She gives most who gives with joy.

– Mother Teresa

Love

Sing about it...   *Write about it...*

Say it with prayer...   *Shout about it...*

Dance it...   *Paint a picture of it...*

Plant a seed...   *Play with a unicorn...*

Build a fort with a child...

Vision

The Power of Seeing

Christina's World

In that brown
and grassy sea,
everything
depends
on her arm,
bony, pink, and turned
just so.

One hand
tethered
irretrievably
to earth's dark knoll.
The other
a sea bird,
broken-winged,
ever seeking
that marvelous,
miraculous
frenzy of flight.

– Gloria Burgess

Vision

The Power of Seeing

Vision is an invisible, yet potent force, connected to our passions and deepest values. A galvanizing vision is a magnet that pulls you toward your desired goal and keeps you headed in the same direction despite the inevitable winds of change.

Vision is at the very core of legacy living. On a personal level, a vision says: *This is who I am, this is what I care about, this is what I am doing about it, and this is where I am headed.* A vision can also include how you are going to get from where you are now to where you want to be. To have pulling *and* staying power, your personal vision must be bigger than you and reach beyond yourself.

On the inspirational path, the covenant of vision involves learning how to see, not just with the outer eye, but with the inner eyes of our heart and soul. Learning about and nurturing our creativity requires us to understand and use the many facets of vision: *perception, intuition, reflection, insight*, and *perspective*.

- *Perception* is how you see things outwardly. Because it is so common, most of us don't think much about perception. We take it for granted. In addition to seeing, perception also includes our awareness of our external environment through our other senses— hearing, smelling, tasting, and touching.

- *Intuition* is your way of perceiving something immediately, without your five senses or your intellectual cognition. It is a way of seeing with eyes of the soul. For creatives, intuition is a time-honored way of knowing. Because intuition results from synthesis rather than analysis, illustrating how we arrived at certain conclusions often requires more time and spaciousness.

- *Reflection* means taking time to look not once but many times at what holds meaning for us. It requires steadfastness, which allows us to hold fast to our vision. Reflection also requires discernment to look at our vision anew, with fresh eyes.

- *Insight* allows us to see and know more deeply what has meaning for us. In her book *Amazing Grace*, Kathleen Norris connects this kind of seeing with revelation, which is at the heart of insight. She reminds us that "Revelation is not explanation, and it is not acquired through reading... It is the revealing of the presence of a God who cares for all creatures."

- *Perspective* is the way in which you see and has everything to do with your vantage point or point of view. Perspective helps you understand your personal vision as it relates to other aspects of your life.

In many cultures, the archetype of vision is called the Visionary, the Creative, or the Artist. This archetype is available to each of us at any time. We invoke this archetype when we use our foresight and hindsight (a way of reflecting), and when we pay attention to our night dreams and day dreams. We invoke this archetype when we engage our energies to bring forth our signature presence.

Michael Gelb and Tony Buzan, leading experts on human performance and creativity, remind us that we are programmed to see what we envision:

> The ability to picture a desired outcome is built into your brain, and your brain is designed through millions of years of evolution to help you succeed in matching that picture with your performance.

Legacy living calls us to envision what we want to create and for whom.

On the inspirational path, vision not only connects us to what we value most deeply, our vision becomes the outward manifestation of what we value. All too often, our values lie beneath the surface, beneath the level of our conscious awareness. But whether we are conscious of our values or not, we manifest them in our patterns of behavior, in our likes and dislikes, in our relationships—in all that we are and do. The ultimate goal is to become conscious of what we care about, so that we can intentionally choose how we direct the precious resources of our time, attention, and energy.

A few months ago, after she had taken her students on a field trip to the Chamber of Commerce, I talked with a middle school teacher about her work. I asked her to describe her work to me. "I am a steward," she told me, "entrusted with preparing our young people to become ambassadors, tribal leaders if you will, in our global village. I take students out of the classroom at least one day each week. These young people have met with our mayor, the City Council, the police chief, women and men in transition centers, docents at the art museum... I encourage them to ask questions, to talk about their goals, to respect and interact with all kinds of people. I

The function of art is to do more than tell it like it is— it's to imagine what's possible.

– bell hooks

want these young people to become knowledgeable, confident citizens and to learn about their community first hand, not just by reading books and logging onto the Internet."

Imagination takes humility, love, and great courage.

– Carson McCullers

Not once did this teacher talk about her role as instructor. She had a vision for her work that went beyond herself and one that was more expansive than our conventional notions of what teachers do. Not only did this teacher have vision, she instilled it in her students as well.

Many of us have heard the following story, which reminds us of the difference between working for the sake of work and working with an intentional sense of vision.

> A monk passing by three men cutting stone stopped to ask them about their work. The monk asked the first stonecutter, "What are you doing?" Without looking up from his work, the first stonecutter replied, "I am cutting stones. Anyone can see that." Then the monk asked the second stonecutter, "What are you doing?" He looked at the monk briefly and replied, "I am cutting stones for a building." The monk asked the third stonecutter, "What are you doing?" The third stonecutter stopped what he was doing, looked at the monk, extended his arms over his head and exclaimed. "Why, I am cutting stones for a cathedral."

How might our work become infused with more attentiveness, appreciation, faith, and vision if we were to re-imagine our work like the monk who envisions a cathedral as the result of his labors? Might we approach work with a renewed sense of invigoration, even zeal? Might we, like the cathedral-minded stonecutter, cross the radiant threshold and enter *kairos* time?

Creating a personal vision for yourself and living with it on a daily basis creates momentum, for vision is a dynamic force that propels us forward. A dynamic vision infuses us with vigor and passion. For just like us, visions are alive, constantly growing and evolving. Though we experience their dynamic force in the present, visions pull us toward the future.

In order to manifest our vision, we must have clarity about it. We must also be able to access the many different facets of vision—*perception*, *intuition*, *reflection*, *insight*, and *perspective*. With clarity about our personal vision and access to its myriad facets, we sharpen what we envision on the whetstones of truth and congruence.

We know that our vision is an expression of our truth when it is aligned with our authentic self. Congruence is a matter of inner and outer alignment. It is what a colleague calls the "one-hat philosophy of life." This means that you wear one hat—the same one—no matter who you are with, no matter where you are. You are the same person with your spouse as with your boss, at the dentist's office or at the dry cleaners, attending a potluck at your community center or attending church.

You know that your personal vision is aligned with your voice and values when you:

- Express yourself without editing what you say or do in the company of both friends and strangers.

- Bring forth your signature presence—your special skills, talents, and abilities that exist nowhere else on the planet.

- Offer your creativity freely—in relationships, at work, and in your community.

- Engage your imagination as a resource and ally to enhance your creativity and in how you use your signature presence.

- Tell yourself and others what's true for you, and act on that truth with passion, purpose, and consistency.

- Spend time to periodically reflect on what's important to ensure you are still in alignment.

- Spend time in solitude to partner and reconnect with your dreams, thoughts, and goals—the elements of your personal vision.

- Feed yourself an ample diet of solitude, for it nourishes the soul and deepens the connection to your inner and outer vision.

- Practice the many ways of seeing:

  ○ Notice and observe what you perceive through your physical experiences.

  ○ Pay attention to your intuition. Honor it at least once a day.

  ○ Reflect on someone or something you care about.

  ○ Pay attention to who and what inspires you.

  ○ Notice what is being revealed to you. What are your insights?

  ○ Practice gently shifting your perspective.

Solitude is the furnace of transformation.

– Henri Nouwen

In solitude, we are silent, so that we may hear, focused so that we may craft substantial things.

– Pam Grout

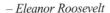

How does this gentle shift alter your personal vision?

○ Subordinate all else to focus exclusively on manifesting your life's purpose. If money were no object, what would you do with the rest of your life?

• Realize that with the help of God you are the only one who can realize your dreams, the only one who can bring your personal vision to fruition.

Invitation

If not now, when? If not you, who?

– adapted from Rabbi Hillel

By expressing vision for someone or something each day, you nurture its inclusion into your natural way of being. Your daily expression of vision will soon become a habit, and a habit becomes a part of you.

I invite you to set aside time each day for the next few weeks to respond to one or more of the questions and activities in the next section "Reflections and Discoveries."

To focus on the covenant of vision, begin by finding or creating a special place in your home, office, or outdoors. This special place is your sanctuary. Your sanctuary is a sacred place, a place of respite and "creative incubation." Your sanctuary can also be a place to say aloud what aspect of vision is most present for you.

There are many ways to make your place of sanctuary special. You might play your favorite music, burn incense, add fresh flowers, or draw inspiration from a photo of a loved one or a favorite quote.

In your place of sanctuary, take a moment to set your intention in this sacred space. I like to light a candle, a time-honored way of bringing light into darkness. Lighting a candle is also a way of honoring precious souls who have crossed over, of focusing our attention on what truly matters.

When I dare to be powerful—to use my strength in the service of my vision, then it becomes less and less important whether I am afraid.

– Audre Lorde

Remember that finding or creating and spending time in your sanctuary is not a luxury. It is an imperative. It is necessary for nurturing your authentic voice, your creative gifts, your signature presence.

———⬦———

Each day, for a week, place an item signifying vision in your sanctuary—a special candle, photo, letter, flower, poem, prayer, ring, incense, or favorite book.

Each time you add a new object or keepsake, take a moment to express aloud what this dimension of vision has offered to you. Giving voice to your vision is a way of em*body*ing it, a way to hold it more deeply in your body's memory.

———⬦———

In your journal or in the space below, I invite you to make a covenant with yourself to express vision for or to someone or something daily.

Reflections and Discoveries

🦋 What does vision mean to you? What is the rhythm of vision in your life?

🦋 As a child, what did you want to be when you grew up? How are you living this vision now?

What lies behind us and what lies before us are tiny matters compared to what lies within us.

– Oliver Wendell Holmes

🦋 Who has inspired you most in your life? What did this person evoke in you?

❧ Who are your heroines and heroes? Why? What qualities do they possess?

❧ Imagine yourself living to your full potential. You're demonstrating all of your talents, enjoying your strengths. You're in your element, performing at your peak. What are you doing? What qualities do you possess? How do you feel about yourself?

❧ What aspirations or talents have you not been using?

❧ Who do you envy? What is it about this person that you envy most? Is this a quality you want to develop in yourself?

❧ In your daydreams and fantasies, where do you spend time?

If the doors of perception were cleansed, we would see the world as it really is, infinite.

— William Blake

❧ If money were no object, where would you go for a month-long retreat?

🎵 Spending time alone nourishes our dreams. How do you invite solitude into your life?

🎵 Imagine yourself one year from now. What do you want to have accomplished by then that you have yet to begin?

I couldn't find anything that truly reflected what I thought was my reality and the reality of other women my age. Since I couldn't find it, the only responsible recourse was to write some myself.

– Ntozake Shange

🎵 What do you need to do to begin? When will you begin?

🎵 Imagine yourself five years from now. What do you want to have accomplished by then that you have yet to begin?

116

🦎 What do you need to do to begin? When will you begin?

🦎 Imagine yourself 10 years from now. What do you want to have accomplished by then that you have yet to begin?

🦎 What do you need to do to begin? When will you begin?

Integrity
The Power of Wholeness

Song to Myself

(excerpt)

It doesn't matter to me
    what you do or where you work.
I want to know
    who you are
    when the sun goes down
    and if you are willing
    to put everything on the line
    to fulfill your soul's desire.
.
.
.

It doesn't matter to me
    that you have a past.
I want to know
    if you will celebrate your present
    if you will take a stand
    declare yourself sing *I am*
    boldly and with rejoicing
    not only to the stars at night
    but to anyone
    anywhere
    without apologies
    or regrets.

– Gloria Burgess

Integrity

The Power of Wholeness

Integrity is connected to *integer*, which means whole. Integrity is concerned with wholeness, truth, authenticity, and health. When we act with integrity, we embrace and honor all aspects of who we are: our adult selves, our youthful selves, and our child-like nature. When we act with integrity, we are also honest with ourselves and others.

Legacy living calls us to walk with integrity. When we walk with integrity, we rejoice in our positive qualities and are able to integrate our less desirable, or so-called shadow, qualities. Walking with integrity encompasses what it means to be human, to be real.

On the inspirational path, the covenant of integrity requires two things of us:

1. Knowing and expressing ourselves wholly. This means not hiding our light under a bush, but bringing all of ourselves with us wherever we are.

2. Expressing our truth, or our authenticity, which means being true to our first nature, being what and who God intended us to be. Sometimes we call this expressing our own true voice.

When we stand in our integrity, we stand in a posture of humility. Derived from *humus*, or ground, we stand in the ground of our being, the very ground of what the soul calls home. To arrive at that place, we must gather and honor the parts of ourselves that we may have kept hidden or that we lost along the way in our journey from childhood into adulthood.

Poet Mary Oliver offers many poems that resonate with the creative, authentic life. Near the beginning of my workshops on creativity and leadership, I often read "The Journey." In this poem Oliver invites us to stand before the mirror and take a hard look at ourselves. Wherever you are along the inspirational path, "The Journey" issues a wake-up call that demands an answer to the question *what are you doing about your life?*

The poem's opening lines capture the stark reality of a life lived in muted and hushed tones, a life that hungers for its own truth, vitality, and boldness.

> *One day you finally knew*
> *What you had to do, and began, ...*

From this point on, as you are drawn deeper and deeper into the poem, you recognize that the journey Oliver describes is not unlike your own. And you encounter not some stranger but your very own self as you arrive at the poem's center.

The Journey

> One day you finally knew
> what you had to do, and began,
> though the voices around you
> kept shouting
> their bad advice—
> though the whole house
> began to tremble
> and you felt the old tug
> at your ankles.
> "Mend my life!"
> each voice cried.

But you didn't stop.
You knew what you had to do,
though the wind pried
with its stiff fingers
at the very foundations,
though their melancholy
was terrible.
It was already late
enough, and a wild night,
and the road full of fallen
branches and stones.
But little by little,
as you left their voices behind,
the stars began to burn
through the sheets of clouds,
and there was a new voice
which you slowly
recognized as your own,
that kept you company
as you strode deeper and deeper
into the world,
determined to do
the only thing you could do—
determined to save
the only life you could save.

As in all work of mythic substance, "The Journey" provides a mirror into which you peer only to see your own face reflected back. Utterly human, you recognize that Oliver is not talking through some disembodied, disinterested third person. As if through some sleight of hand, Oliver's words become your own words.

If you are faithful to your own experience, you recognize the voices "shouting their bad advice" as the voices of people you know—your parents, teachers, or friends. Their advice may have been well intended, but not in keeping with who you are or who you must become. Trembling and pulled, like the poem's speaker, you realize that you must stride from tender and fragile to courageous and triumphant, choosing life—your own salvation—over certain death.

In her poem "Anima," Ellen Wehle echoes this theme of journeying from caution and fear to conscious determination and salvation.

> … A hundred times we betray our lives and did you think no one was listening? Make no mistake: the record is kept, the tally is known and with tails of fire all your past choices are hurtling across the sky, your own face, mouth open, lit in fear and longing. Who will save you now from the wages of your caution?

On the inspirational path, integrity invites us not only to quest after our own true voice, but also to fully embrace our whole selves. Only in that embrace can we become lit, not in fear and longing but in passion and satisfaction. Only in that embrace can we pay the wages not of our caution but of our courageousness.

The process of becoming whole takes time and seasoning; indeed, integration—the journey toward wholeness—is the work of a lifetime. As human beings, we cannot become whole until we recognize, honor, and embrace all of who we are.

Most of us are not very fond of our shadowy parts. We would much rather be known for our goodness and kindness, our courageous and heroic natures. Even the best of us sometimes have thoughts or behave in ways that we later question,

The right way to wholeness is through fitful starts and wrong turnings.

– Carl Jung

For the artist what and how are one.

– William McElcheran

125

embarrass us, or make us ashamed. It is through our less than honorable actions that we learn more deeply who we really are. It is by traveling to the dark, shadowy places in our nature that we return with more knowledge and, if we are lucky, greater wisdom, discovering more deeply the ground of our being. For if we can recognize the inevitable darkness in our own soul, we can claim that darkness as our own rather than projecting it onto others.

When Thomas Moore writes about artistic creativity and the necessity of owning our shadows, he writes about each of us.

> Creativity finds its soul when it embraces its shadow. The artist's block, for instance, is a well-known part of the creative process: inspiration stops and the writer is faced with an intractable empty page. Everyone, not only artists, recognizes that evaporation of the page. A mother may enjoy raising her children for months or years, every day thinking up new ideas for them. Then one day the inspiration leaves and emptiness takes over. If we could see how our blank spots are a part of our creativity, we might not so quickly exclude this aspect of our work from our humble lives.

Another aspect of becoming whole is to acknowledge, claim, and revel in our childlike qualities. When we are open to surprise, awe, and wonder, we can see with new eyes, with younger eyes, with the eyes of a child. When we make way for the inevitable mistakes in our life, we do not become blocked or stuck. Instead we free up energy that is better used elsewhere. And if we do experience blocks, we are more open to their rhythms and the

I am inexorably drawn to shadows. When I am among them, my understanding deepens.

– Anne Lamott

You've got to keep the child alive; you can't create without it.

– Joni Mitchell

126

antidotes of play, laughter, and leisure. When we make a place for these carefree realms, we open the door to the sanctity of spontaneity, liberation, and joy, those qualities of childhood that yearn to be honored in our busy adult lives.

What artist Wassily Kandinsky observes about painting applies to those who paint as well as to the rest of us. "In every painting a whole is mysteriously enclosed, a whole life of tortures, doubts, and hours of enthusiasm and inspiration." It is our tortures and doubts together with our enthusiasms and inspirations that make us complete, that make us radiant jewels in the eyes and crown of our Creator.

Each of us can benefit by knowing ourselves, being true to ourselves, and bringing our whole selves forward. We can learn much from individual study. But individual study alone yields an incomplete picture of who we are. We can also learn from trusted friends, family members, and mentors. These important allies can shine the light on our diversity, showing us dimensions that we may not fully recognize as strengths or growing edges. Like mirrors, trusted friends, family members, and mentors can reflect qualities that may be obscured or hidden from us.

What the caterpillar calls the end of the world, the master calls a butterfly.

– Richard Bach

Invitation

If not now, when? If not you, who?

– adapted from Rabbi Hillel

Art, prayer, and healing: all come from the same source—the human soul. The energy that fuels these processes is the basic force of life, of creativity, of love.

– Anna Halprin

By expressing integrity for someone or something each day, you nurture its inclusion into your natural way of being. Your daily expression of integrity will soon become a habit, and a habit becomes a part of you.

I invite you to set aside time each day for the next few weeks to respond to one or more of the questions and activities in the next section "Reflections and Discoveries."

To focus on the covenant of integrity, begin by finding or creating a special place in your home, office, or outdoors. This special place is your sanctuary. Your sanctuary is a sacred place, a place of respite and "creative incubation." Your sanctuary can also be a place to say aloud what aspect of integrity is most present for you.

There are many ways to make your place of sanctuary special. You might play your favorite music, burn incense, add fresh flowers, or draw inspiration from a photo of a loved one or a favorite quote.

In your place of sanctuary, take a moment to set your intention in this sacred space. I like to light a candle, a time-honored way of bringing light into darkness. Lighting a candle is also a way of honoring precious souls who have crossed over, of focus-

ing our attention on what truly matters.

Remember that finding or creating and spending 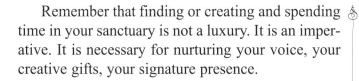 time in your sanctuary is not a luxury. It is an imperative. It is necessary for nurturing your voice, your creative gifts, your signature presence.

———◇———

Each day, for a week, place an item signifying integrity in your sanctuary—a special candle, photo, letter, flower, poem, prayer, ring, incense, or favorite book.

Each time you add a new object or keepsake, take a moment to express aloud what this dimension of integrity has offered to you. Giving voice to your integrity is a way of em*body*ing it, a way to hold it more deeply in your body's memory.

———◇———

In your journal or in the space below, make a covenant with yourself to express integrity to or for someone or something daily.

Reflections and Discoveries

🎵 What does integrity mean to you? What is the rhythm of integrity in your life?

🎵 What stories do you enjoy telling about yourself? Do you tell the whole story, or do you edit parts of it?

🎵 What stories are you embarrassed or ashamed to tell yourself? What are you embarrassed to talk about with friends? With family? With loved ones?

❧ What stories have you never told anyone about yourself?

❧ Imagine your favorite flower or animal. What makes it complete? Would it be the same with one, two, or more parts missing?

❧ What parts of you are missing or muted?

Resistance to tyrants is obedience to God.

– Thomas Jefferson

❧ Draw a picture of yourself with missing or muted parts.

❧ Draw a picture of yourself, whole, as God intended you to be.

.

❧ Imagine that you have just completed writing a book about yourself—the whole of who you are. Give your book a title.

It is good to have an end to journey towards, but it is the journey that matters in the end.

– Ursula Le Guin

Staying on the Inspirational Path

If we did what we are capable of doing, we would astound ourselves.

– Thomas Edison

I hope that *Legacy Living* has encouraged you to get off the bank of the river and to "wade in the water," to move from the shallows and delve into the depths of your own magnificence and creativity. I also hope it has inspired you to stand in the full radiance of who you are, to bring forth your signature presence, and encouraged you to be more intentional about the legacy you are creating.

Whenever we engage our creative energies, we release enchantment and magic into the world. We participate in a potent and energizing process that reaffirms, restores, and replenishes us and those around us. We honor the past and say *yes* to the present and the future.

But whatsoever of the holy kingdom Was in the power of memory to treasure Will be my theme until the song is ended.

– Dante Alighieri

Legacy living calls us to make a covenant with ourselves to bring forth our signature presence. Making this covenant is a way of saying *yes* to God and *yes* to transformation—our own and whatever change we envision for others.

Legacy living is an invitation to wear your soul on the outside, to step fully into the power of your signature presence, to let your creative spirit take flight and soar! As you become more intimate with your signature presence, remember to express some aspect of it daily. Some days you might simply say "thank you" to yourself or a friend, utter a prayer, recount a blessing—expressing the covenant of *gratitude*. On another day you might offer a word of encouragement, nurture a seed, constant in your devotion to someone or something that has yet to manifest—expressing the covenant of *faith*.

Legacy living is not a luxury. It is an imperative. Spread joy and legacy by passing on the blessings of your journey with friends and loved ones. Start small. Keep a legacy journal. Rather than buy a journal, make one. Personalize it. Decorate its covers using your favorite colors. Clip and use pictures and words from your favorite magazines. Make it yours from cover to cover. Start a legacy circle. Use your legacy journal with others in your legacy circle.

If you wait for tomorrow, tomorrow comes. If you don't wait for tomorrow, tomorrow comes.

– Senegalese Proverb

———◈———

Remember the promise and power of each covenant.

- *Legacy* offers the power of stewardship. Be conscious about your legacy. Create for someone else something that will have an enduring impact.

- *Gratitude* offers the power of blessing. Counting your blessings opens your heart, enabling you to draw more deeply from the wellspring of your creativity.

- *Faith* offers the power of unshakable devotion. Be faithful to yourself even when it appears as though nothing is happening. Something is, and everything awaits you.

- *Love* offers the power of passion. Let your curiosity lead you, then follow your passion. Take a chance: take note of what gives you energy and vitality. Passion is the doorway to your purpose and promise.

- *Vision* offers the power of seeing—inwardly and outwardly. Take time to envision and reflect on what matters most deeply to you.

- *Integrity* offers the power of wholeness. Know yourself. Be true to yourself. Stand and walk with integrity. Express the beauty and bounty of who you are.

This book is not the end, it's a beginning. Continue using this book as a resource for inspiration. Review the suggested readings and other resources near the end of this book, and take time to add resources of your own.

Sources

Unless otherwise noted in the chapter in which they appear, the poems and opening reflections for each chapter were written by the author.

The author and publisher acknowledge permission to use and reprint previously published works. Diligent efforts were made to obtain permission to reprint poems and other selections from previously published works. Upon notification, omissions will be included in future reprints.

Suggested Readings and Other Resources

The resources listed here are only a beginning. To make this list really sing, make it yours by adding resources of your own. Share your ideas with friends, loved ones, and co-workers. Share them with me. I welcome your ideas and your stories of triumph, joy, and encouragement. Even the inevitable disappointments. Write to me at *gloria@jazz-inc.com*.

Amazing Grace: A Vocabulary of Faith, Kathleen Norris

An Altar of Words: Wisdom, Comfort, and Inspiration for African-American Women, Byllye Avery

Art and Healing: Using Expressive Art to Heal Your Body, Mind, and Spirit, Barbara Ganim

Artist's Way, The, Julia Cameron

Bird by Bird, Anne Lamott

Blue Fire, A: The Essential Writings of James Hillman, edited by Thomas Moore

Book of Psalms, The Bible

Care of the Soul: A Guide To Cultivating Depth and Sacredness in Everyday Life, Thomas Moore

Courage to Create, The, Rollo May

Courage to Teach, The, Parker Palmer

Creating, Robert Fritz

"Creating a Shared Vision," Gloria J. Burgess

Creative Spirit, The, Daniel Goleman

Creativity and the Soul of Leadership, (Audio), Gloria J. Burgess

Fingerpainting on the Moon: Writing and Creativity as a Path to Freedom, Peter Levitt

Forty Ways to Say I Love You, James R. Bjorge

Four Agreements, The, Don Miguel Ruiz

Glimpses of Grace, Madeleine L'Engle

God Is At Eye Level: Photography As A Healing Art, Jan Phillips

Healing Wisdom of Africa, The: Finding Life Purpose Through Nature, Ritual, & Community, Malidoma Patrice Somé

Heart Aroused, The: Poetry and the Preservation of the Soul in Corporate America, David Whyte

Heart of A Woman, The, Maya Angelou

Heart of Business, The, (Film), Across Borders Media

Heroine's Journey, The, Maureen Murdoch

How to Think Like Leonardo da Vinci, Michael Gelb

I Dream a World, Brian Lanker

I Hope You Dance, (Book and CD), Lee Ann Womack

In the Spirit, Susan L. Taylor

Journey of the Rose, (Book and CD), Gloria Burgess; original music by John Burgess

Let Your Life Speak, Parker Palmer

Life's Companion: Journal Writing as a Spiritual Quest, Christina Baldwin

Living Your Creativity Every Day, Gloria J. Burgess

Marry Your Muse: Making a Lasting Commitment to Your Creativity, Jan Phillips

Meditations, Thomas Moore

Nobel Prize Acceptance Speech, William Faulkner

Open Door, The, Gloria Burgess

Path of Least Resistance, The: Learning to Become the Creative Force in Your Own Life, Robert Fritz

"Praying on Paper," *Christian Century*, Stephanie Paulsell

Prophet, The, Kahlil Gibran

"Reflection As a Key Leadership Practice," Gloria J. Burgess

Soul's Code, The, James Hillman

Soul Is Here for Its Own Joy, The, edited by Robert Bly

Soul Mapping, An Imaginative Way to Self-Discovery, Nina H. Frost, Kenneth C. Ruge, and Richard W. Shoup

Spiritual Literacy, Frederic and Mary Ann Brussat

Stand for Children, Marian Wright Edelman

Stirring the Waters: Writing to Find Your Spirit, Jannell Moon

Ten Poems That Will Change Your Life, Roger Housden

Trust the Process: An Artist's Guide to Letting Go, Shaun McNiff

Wild Seed, The, Li-Young Lee

Woman's Book of Creativity, The, C. Diane Ealy

www.jazz-inc.com – Tips for Living Your Creativity Every Day, Gloria J. Burgess

Additional Resources

Add your own readings and other resources here.

About the Author

Gloria J. Burgess, PhD, distinguished scholar in performance studies, is an award-winning writer, director, and performing artist. Dr. Burgess is also a leadership consultant and executive coach. A sought-after speaker, she presents inspirational keynotes and leads workshops worldwide, sharing her passion for leadership, creativity, and legacy living.

Dr. Burgess delivers keynotes, presentations, and artistic performances for corporate, civic, school, and charitable organizations. Her clients include the International Coach Federation, Microsoft, MSNBC, Boeing, University of Washington, Association for Quality Management, Girl Scouts of America, International Society for Technical Communication, Skagit River Poetry Festival, Robert Wood Johnson Foundation, Helene Fuld Trust, Casey Family Programs, The Friends of Third Place Commons, Experience Music Project, and The Lift Every Voice Foundation.

A Cave Canem Poetry Fellow, Dr. Burgess has published three volumes of poetry: *The Open Door*, *Journey of the Rose*, and *A Yellow Wood*. She has also produced and recorded a CD of poetry and original music and has written an inspirational picture book for children of all ages about her father's life-changing relationship with writer William Faulkner.

For more information on keynotes, programs, performances, workshops, and products, visit Dr.

Burgess's web site: *www.jazz-inc.com*. You can write to her at:

> Gloria J. Burgess
> c/o Jazz, Inc.
> 7500 – 212th Street SW
> Edmonds, Washington 98026-7618

Appreciations

Our life's purpose is most profoundly demonstrated in how we live and by the legacy we leave. I am grateful to the countless women and men who have left enduring legacies of their creative spirit, for I stand on their broad shoulders. I am also grateful for the women and men who have thought deeply and persistently about creativity and its myriad expressions. I especially appreciate the individuals cited in this book: I thank each of you for your words of wisdom and inspiration, for daring to wear your soul on the outside.

Dante Alighieri
Byllye Avery • Richard Bach
Christina Baldwin • Ysaye Barnwell • Melody
Beattie • Wendy Beckett • Mary McLeod Bethune
Denise Bissonnette • William Blake • Sarah Ban Breathnach
Gwendolyn Brooks • Emily Barrett Browning • John Burroughs
Tony Buzan • Julia Cameron • Joseph Campbell • Hodding Carter
Shirley Chisholm • Joan Chittister • Cicero • e. e. cummings • Max DePree
Meister Eckhardt • Marian Wright Edelman • Thomas Edison • Albert Einstein
T. S. Eliot • Ralph Waldo Emerson • Adolfo Pérez Esquivel • Mari Evans • William
Faulkner • Nikky Finney • St. Francis • Robert Frost • Johannes Gaertner • Michael
Gelb • Kahlil Gibran • Mary Jane Gillespie • Johann W. von Goethe • Martha Graham
Pam Grout • Ann Halprin • Joy Harjo • Robert Hayden • Seamus Heaney • Rabbi
Hillel • Oliver Wendell Holmes • bell hooks • Langston Hughes • John James Ingalls
William James • Thomas Jefferson • June Jordan • Carl Jung • Franz Kafka
Wassily Kandinsky • King David • Martin Luther King, Jr. • Jacob Lawrence • Madeleine
L'Engle • Ursula Le Guin • Linda Schierse Leonard • Anne Morrow Lindbergh • Audre
Lorde • John Lubbock • Benjamin Mays • Carson McCullers • William McElcheran
Earnest McEwen, Jr. • Mildred McEwen • Margaret Mead • Thomas Merton • Joni
Mitchell • Thomas Moore • Mark Nepo • Kathleen Norris • Henry Nouwen • Naomi
Shihab Nye • John O'Donohue • Mary Oliver • Parker Palmer • St. Paul • Pablo
Picasso • Plato • Marcel Proust • Arlene Raven • Pamela Reeve Reese • Eleanor
Roosevelt • Don Miguel Ruiz • Jalal-al-Din-Rumi • M. J. Ryan • Camille Saint-
Saens • Florida Maxwell Scott • Ntozake Shange • Bill Shore • Sydney
Smith • William Stafford • Carol Staudacher • Gertrude Stein
Mother Teresa • Yi-Fu Tuan • Desmond Tutu • Henry Vaughn
Patrice Vecchione • Derek Walcott • Ellen Wehle
David Whyte • Nancy Willard • Betty Williams
William Carlos Williams
Marion Woodman

I also express gratitude for world proverbs from persons and peoples whose wisdom and traditions have been passed on orally for thousands of years and in writing for several hundred.